KILLERS IN AFRICA

The Truth About Animals Lying in Wait and Hunters Lying in Print

Alexander Lake in Africa in 1922 Unknown Photographer

KILLERS IN AFRICA
The Truth About Animals Lying in Wait and Hunters Lying in Print

Alexander Lake

**THE RESNICK LIBRARY
OF AFRICAN ADVENTURE**
Mike Resnick, Series Editor

ALEXANDER Books
Founded 332 B.C.
a division of Creativity, Inc.
65 Macedonia Road
Alexander, NC 28701 USA
(704) 255-8719

Publisher: Ralph Roberts
Vice-President/Operations: Pat Hutchison Roberts
Executive Editor: Susie McDonald

Resnick Library of African Adventure
Series Editor: Mike Resnick

Editors: Lorna Bolkey, Pat Hutchison Roberts,
        Joshua P. Warren, Susie McDonald

Cover Design: **WorldComm®**
Interior Design & Electronic Page Assembly: **WorldComm®**
Photographs (unless otherwise indicated) by Carol Resnick
Cover Photo: Corel Professional Photos CD-ROM

Copyright ©1951, 1952, 1953 Alexander Lake.
Copyright ©1995 Storm Lake. All rights reserved.
Introduction Copyright © 1995 Mike Resnick.

Reproduction and translation of any part of this work beyond that permitted by Sections 107 and 108 of the United States Copyright Act without the permission of the copyright owners is unlawful. Printed in the United States of America.

10 9 8 7 6 5 4 3 2 1

ISBN 1-57090-013-2

Library of Congress: 95-078530

The author and publisher have made every effort in the preparation of this book to ensure the accuracy of the information. However, the information in this book is sold without warranty, either express or implied. Neither the author's estate nor Alexander Books will be liable for any damages caused or alleged to be caused directly, indirectly, incidentally, or consequentially by the information in this book.

The opinions expressed in this book are solely those of the author and are not necessarily those of Alexander Books.

Alexander Books—a division of Creativity, Inc.—is a full–service publisher located at 65 Macedonia Road, Alexander NC 28701. Phone (704) 252–9515, Fax (704) 255–8719. For orders only: 1-800-472-0438. Visa and MasterCard accepted.

CONTENTS

Introduction 7

1. Debunking African Hunting 13

2. Lions 29

3. Elephants 47

4. Baboons 65

5. Rhinos 85

6. Crocodiles 105

7. More Lions 135

8. More Baboons 155

9. Buffalo 171

10. Snakes 191

11. Hippos 209

12. Antelope 229

13. More Antelope 245

14. Leopards 259

African Elephants

INTRODUCTION
by Mike Resnick

There have been five great American writers on the subject of Africa. Two of them, Ernest Hemingway and Robert Ruark, are more famous for their fiction, and remain in print all over the world today. A third, former president Theodore Roosevelt, wrote just one book about Africa, the classic *African Game Trails*; it is not only an excellent book in itself, but because of who its author was, it has remained in print for three-quarters of a century. The fourth, Peter Hathaway Capstick, is the most recent of the batch, and is still producing excellent books about Africa for St. Martin's Press and various other publishers; all of his work is still available.

The fifth—and quite possibly the best of them, at least when writing about Africa—was Alexander Lake. Strangely enough, none of his work is in print, a situation that will be corrected with the publication of this edition of **Killers In Africa**.

Lake was a big game hunter, but a hunter with a difference. At a time—the late 1940s and early 1950s—when one hunter after another was selling macho yarns filled to overflowing with false bravado, Lake began debunking all the myths that had been making the rounds. Indeed, when **Killers In Africa** was compiled and published, the advertising catch-phrase was *"The truth about animals lying in wait and hunters lying in print!"*

It wasn't so far from wrong, either. Perhaps the most famous lions in history are the notorious Man-Eaters of Tsavo. Lt.-Col. J. H. Patterson made a literary career out of recounting his adventures with the beasts. It takes Lake less than half of the first chapter of this book to point out every single thing Patterson did wrong, and to point out what he *should* have done had he any understanding of African lions, which he admittedly lacked.

Lake himself knew Africa intimately. He hunted early enough so that he was not confined to just one country but indeed covered the entire continent, and his clientele was more colorful and memorable than any of the animals he hunted—one of the reasons why his books were so popular when they came out 40 years ago. He knew that people are more interesting than any animals, even man-eaters.

He was one of the first to suggest that there's nothing lower on the scale of humanity than a man who would kill a gorilla. He was the first to point out that, far from having to shoot a rhino when it charges, it's just as easy to dance aside, since once it lowers its head it's virtually blind. He remains the only hunter who argues that hunting antelope is more difficult and more satisfying than hunting the Big Five.

Not much is known of Lake's life, compared to

Selous or Karamojo Bell or some of the more famous hunters. We do know that he was born in Chicago on July 29, 1893, the oldest son of a Methodist minister, and that he went with his family to South Africa in 1908, where his father was not only a missionary but also performed extremely dangerous work for the British Parliament in matters pertaining to slave labor conditions in the Belgian Congo.

He attended the Marist Brothers College in Johannesburg, where he was the captain of the rifle team that represented the Transvaal in the All-British Empire Shumaker Cup. He set a record of 10 bull's-eyes in 11 seconds, which brought him to the attention of Nicobar Jones, one of the earliest licensed guides in Africa and one of the Dark Continent's most capable hunters. Jones hired him as a meat hunter when he turned 18 years old, in 1911; his duties were to supply game to transport wagon trains which in turn supplied mines and railroad builders in Portugese East Africa, Northern Rhodesia, German Southwest Africa, Tanganyika, Kenya and Uganda. He soon became an expert spoorer and hunter of all types of game, especially antelope.

Lake apprenticed under Jones, who taught him all the tricks of the trade, and eventually became a hunter in his own right, assisted by his unsurpassed Zulu tracker, Ubusuku. He refused to be associated with any of the groups of professional hunters that had begun organizing in Kenya and Tanganyika. He was bitterly opposed to "rocking chair safaris" that took tourist hunters to the game, approached the animals by truck, and permitted the so-called hunters to fire in perfect safety. He also did what he could to stop the elephant poaching in Tanganyika, but without much success.

He became fascinated with animals' habits and temperaments, and studied them both as a hunter and a naturalist. His numerous articles were published in the *Rand Daily Mail* and the *London Daily Mail*. He also wrote extensively about the various tribes he encountered, and these writings were incorporated in his father's reports to the British.

When World War I came along, he left Africa to join the American forces in Europe as a pilot, engaging in numerous dogfights above the battlefields. Then it was back to Africa, where he guided hunting parties from all over the world.

He returned to the United States in the 1920s and put his writing experience to good use, hiring on as a reporter and later an editor with the *Spokane Chronicle*, the *Seattle Star*, the *Vancouver World*, and the *San Francisco Examiner*.

Still in love with Africa, Lake returned there during the latter half of the 1930s, then came back to the States, moving to the Mojave Desert where he set up shop as a writer. His African reminiscences never appeared in the "hairy-chested" men's magazines that reveled in close calls and animal body counts, but rather in *Field and Stream* and *Argosy* and a handful of other magazines that would, with his help, bring big-game hunting kicking and screaming into the second half of the 20th Century. As his fame increased, he also started selling to such major markets as *Look*, *Colliers*, and *Reader's Digest*.

This book, obviously pieced together from a number of his magazine articles, covers the animals he hunted, species by species. Each chapter has the feel of a reminiscence told round a campfire, while clearing the dust from your throat with some brandy after a hard day's foot-slogging after animals who were too elusive, or too small, or just too damned pretty, to shoot. And whatever you think of big game hunting (and remember, this was written four decades ago, when attitudes were different—although even then, Lake's favorite clients were those "who know what trophies they want, bag them, and do no other killing except for food"), I think you'll find it almost impossible not to like Lake himself and wish that you could have met him long enough to hear him recount some of his favorite stories.

Killers in Africa appeared in 1953, and immediately made the bestseller list. A year later, Lake produced a second book, also a composite of his articles. Alternately titled **Hunter's Choice** (the American version, also reprinted by Alexander Books) or **African Adventure** (the British version), it's a delightful hodge-podge that covers everything from solving a murder in the Belgian Congo, to getting a pack of apes drunk in order to capture them, to a long and fascinating chapter about how to cook in the bush—everything from roasting impala steaks to making ostrich egg omelets to smoking hippo hams — all told in the same friendly, informal, across-the-campfire style as this book.

Lake's expertise even brought him work as a writer and consultant for Sol Lesser, producer of the Tarzan movies. Continuing to write from his oceanside home, his final years were devoted to extensive research on his father's missionary work, which led him to write two more bestsellers, **Your Prayers Are Always Answered** and **You Need Never Walk Alone**. He died on Christmas Day, 1961, while working on **The Axe and the Cross,** a biography of his father, Dr. John G. Lake.

I don't know how many other readers Lake influenced, but he was certainly the one who got me interested in Africa when I was just a boy. I've been visiting it (six non-hunting safaris thus far) and making a living off of it (13 books and 19 short stories—and if you think it's easy to write that much *science fiction* about Africa, give it a try sometime) ever since.

In my life, I have written three fan letters to writers whose work I deeply admired. One of them, science fiction writer Barry Malzberg, has become my closest friend and occasional collaborator. The second, mystery writer/humorist Ross Spencer, also became a good friend. The third was Alexander Lake, who died a month before my letter could reach him. I consider him a close friend whom I simply never had the good fortune to meet or correspond with, and I hope he would be pleased, if not with the books and stories he inspired, then at least with my bringing **Killers In Africa** back into print for a new generation to enjoy.

DEBUNKING AFRICAN HUNTING

JOHN P. WHORTER, a Colorado mining man, came to Africa to hunt big game. One September morning in 1937 he came face to face with a male lion. Whorter, an excellent shot and as cool as an ice cube, whipped his rifle to his shoulder. His aim was true. But he made one "little" mistake. Two seconds later he was dead, with the lion's fangs buried in his skull.

Whorter's mistake was one of ignorance. He aimed at the center of the hair mass on the lion's head. And that's exactly where the bullet went—smack through the middle of that magnificent mop. Whorter didn't know that a lion has practically no forehead—that the hair on its head is nothing but hair.

In 1925, Peter (Bud) Jones, a Tanganyika rancher, got fed up with the depredations of a rogue elephant that had been playing havoc with the bean fields of the *shamba*. Jones took a .303 rifle and went after that elephant. They met face to face. The elephant, mouth open, trunk raised, charged like a souped-up bulldozer. Jones's shot tore into the back of the roof of the tusker's mouth. A deadly shot, even with a .303 Yet Jones had made one "little" mistake. Ten seconds later he was dead.

Jones's mistake was one of carelessness. When he picked up his rifle he assumed it was loaded with soft-nosed bullets. He didn't look. His aim was true, but a steel-jacketed bullet plowed somewhere close to the elephant's brain, doing little immediate harm. Had that bullet been a soft-nosed one, it would have fattened on impact and shattered the brain instantly.

An Italian trophy hunter named Galli couldn't resist a shot at a rhino one morning. He let loose with a soft-nosed bullet that spattered against the rhino's flank without penetrating. The rhino went berserk, barged head on into a thorn tree, charged at his shadow, then began plowing the ground furiously with his horn. Finally the pain-maddened animal disappeared into heavy brush along the side of a stream. Galli went into the brush after him. Within minutes Galli was a crushed corpse. He, too, had made a "little" mistake.

Galli's mistake was one of foolishness. A wounded rhino will charge anything. The beast is fast and furious, but he doesn't see well, and in the open anyone can side-step a charge. In brush or reeds there is no place to dodge, and the rhino, whose sense of smell is as keen as his eyesight is poor, winds his victim—and that's that.

Hundreds of *professional* hunters have faced situations identical with those that proved fatal to Whorter, Jones, and Galli, but I never knew of one who died because of them. In fact, I've never known a seasoned professional hunter to be killed by any big game in Africa except through carelessness.

To a hunter who knows their habits, there are no really dangerous animals in Africa. Certainly not lions, nor rhinos, nor gorillas; not wildebeest, hippos, nor leopards. I might hedge a little when it comes to buffalo, but not much. If any African animal is to be listed as dangerous, it should be the buffalo, for when wounded, he's vindictive and determined. He'll kill you if he gets a chance.

Around 1910, in my early hunting days, a professional hunter named Spring was tossed, then trampled to death by a buffalo he'd wounded five days before. After being hit, the buffalo circled wide and ambushed Spring along the trail. The animal had chosen a spot for his attack where the trail narrowed down between walls of hooked thorn bushes. Spring, of course, had known of the buffalo's habit of sometimes lying in wait for his victim, but evidently underestimated the animal's long memory. Carelessness.

I might hedge a bit on elephants, too, under certain conditions.

Every year Africa is invaded by hordes of big-game hunters. Some of them are real sportsmen, but some have only a yen to cut loose with a gun. They blaze away at anything they see—monkeys, baboons, antelope, zebras, giraffes, lions, ostriches—leaving behind bloody trails of wounded and slaughtered animals.

Their capacity for doing idiotic things often leads to injury and death to themselves. They pull at the leg of a wounded kudu and have their guts ripped open by slashing hoofs. They walk close to a wounded wildebeest that's playing possum, and are bowled heels over head when the animal leaps snorting to its feet and dashes off like a bat out of hell.

They miss a couple of shots at a lion, terrify him further by screaming and shouting, then instead of standing and shooting it out, they run when the brute charges. They wander near a group of emotionally unstable baboons lined up on a narrow cliff ledge, take a shot at one, and are torn to shreds when the whole troop goes suddenly and violently insane. They wade into rivers without first beating the water with a pole to frighten away crocodiles, and are grabbed by one of the stinking beasts. They wound the shortsighted rhino and stay upwind from him so he'll have no trouble locating them by smell. They get between a hippo and water, not knowing that a hippo shut off from water sometimes goes mad with fear.

Such hunters get lost and starve in a world filled with edible ants, lizards, monkeys, snakes, locusts, slugs, snails, and the inside bark of many trees.

This type of big-game hunter practically commits suicide. The blame is placed on animals that in almost every case wanted nothing but to escape.

Some professionals who guide these big-game tourists just can't take it. They blow up and "bush" their employers for days at a time. There's nothing quite so hapless, helpless, and hopeless as "hunters" who think they are lost.

In contrast, nothing pleases a professional guide and hunter more than to get a job working for a group of true sportsmen. It's also pleasant to work with "bring-'em-back-alive" and "shoot-'em-with-a-camera" hunters. These men and women know animals and frequently take chances that would turn the average sadistic blood-letter into a nervous wreck.

It's pleasant to work with men who know what trophies they want, bag them, and do no other killing except for food. They stalk game carefully, often expertly, and try not to merely wound a beast. Usually they give the animals more than an even break and are happiest when their trophies are won with all odds in favor of the animals.

I suppose most persons who have hunted big game in Africa go home and write articles or books about their adventures. The writings of real sportsmen are factual, while those of the other type are a hodgepodge of fancy, fable, and fabrication.

So far as I know, the United States is the only country in which magazines still publish old, exploded myths about African animals. I'm not referring to hunting and fishing magazines, which make no pretense of publishing nature stuff, but to magazines purporting to publish "true" stories only. An outdoor editor of one such magazine actually has his African animal articles checked for authenticity by British and Belgian propaganda and publicity bureaus whose business it is to foster animal myths as tourist bait. One American magazine that has led the fight against phony African animal stuff is *Argosy*. Another is *Field and Stream* There are others, too, of course, but these two are doing an outstanding job.

For years some magazines in America have had a weakness for stories about man-eating lions.

Man-eaters!

The mangy, tick-scourged, lazy, and usually meek lion does, like a starving wolf or, for that matter, a starving man, sometimes kill and eat a human.

Feed a starving lion and you no longer have a man-eater. Therein lies the tragedy of lions who have killed more than one man because of hunger. They could have been kept from further attacks by being fed an occasional sheep, goat, pig, or antelope until an opportunity came for shooting them.

Most man-eaters are old lions who have lost their teeth and the stamina necessary to knock down a zebra or other food. However, even young lions have turned man-eater at times in areas where the tsetse fly or severe drought has killed off or driven away their normal food supply. Females sometimes attack humans when their young are starving. But authentic stories of man-eaters are rare.

A professional hunter called in to hunt down a man-eater will usually get him within a couple of days. A novice on the same job can play hell.

Back in 1900, two female man-eaters were killed by Lieutenant Colonel J. H. Patterson, a construction engineer on the then-building Uganda Railroad. He had a work crew of several thousand Indian coolies. Before Patterson succeeded in bagging the two animals, they'd devoured twenty-nine of the coolies and had maintained a reign of terror and hysteria that lasted nine long months.

About the only good thing that can be said about Patterson's campaign against the lions is that he showed lots of courage. Aside from that, almost every move he made was either wrong or botched.

This was before my time, of course, but I know the story as well as if I'd been there. I got it straight from Nicobar Jones, an American who for almost fifty years was one of Africa's most expert hunters. Jones is the man who taught me most of what I know about hunting. He was from Ohio, and often in the light of flickering campfires he'd speak of a girl back home who'd worn a pink gingham dress and whose braids of yellow hair shimmered in the sunlight. Jones was always going home next year. He never did. Africa had a hold on him that he couldn't break.

He saw beauty everywhere. I've seen him stand watching a flowing arc of leaping springbok (impala), muttering, "Purty! Purty!" until the last of the herd had disappeared, then plod back to camp, meatless and hungry. Everything in Africa was "purty" to Jones—the sky, the veldt, the forest, morning and night, killers and sunset, rain and wind, a loping lion, a galloping giraffe—everything.

Here's the way Jones told me the story of Colonel Patterson and the man-eaters. We were sitting beside the fire one night watching the shadowy form of a prowling lion just beyond the edge of the firelight. From time to time its eyes flashed green-red in the blackness. Its scent, growling, snarling, and coughing had made the oxen so nervous that they were moaning. The Kaffirs at the other fire were restless and worried. Jones said:

"'Tain't natural for a lion to stay upwind, and 'tain't natural for one to make so much noise when he's stalking. He's just tryin' to panic the oxen, or maybe one of the dogs, so they'll break for the downwind side where maybe four or five of his pals are waiting quietly. Lions ain't much for brains as a rule, but they can be purty smart when they're hungry.

"One night up around Tsavo, inland a bit from Mombasa, a female lion walked into a coolie camp on the railroad and pulled one of the coolies out of his blankets. Instead of eating him close to where she'd grabbed him, like they generally do, she dragged him off into the brush. About the same time, another female lion showed up on the opposite side of the camp and got herself a coolie too.

"Take them coolies now. They ain't got any guts. There was about three thousand of them in that camp, more or less, but they let them two lions live off them for the biggest part of a year.

"Anyway, when they told Colonel Patterson about the two men bein' dragged off, he didn't believe it. Thought they'd deserted. But when a third coolie was jerked from his tent and his partially eaten body was found close to camp, the colonel got busy. Trouble was, he was new to Africa.

"He built himself a lion trap. He made a big box out of wood and iron, and fixed the door so it'd shut fast when a spring in the floor was stepped on. Patterson built bars across one end of the box, sort of fencing off a small room, and in that room he put a couple of coolies for bait. Nothing happened, and after while the trap was abandoned.

"Months later one of the man-eaters came across the trap and went inside to sniff around. The door swung shut, and there was man-eater Number One smack in the condemned cage. Her roars brought Patterson and a bunch of armed coolies on the run. They turned loose a fusillade of shots, missed the lion, but blasted off the iron bar across the door. The lion beat it with bullets buzzing past her ears.

"For a time Patterson spent his days crawling on hands and knees through dense thorn thickets. Several times he got so tangled up that coolies had to untangle him. I guess he thought he was huntin' lions, but—well, he was new to the country.

"Them lions kept grabbing off a coolie every ten days or so. They were seen and shot at plenty. Waste of bullets. Patterson himself missed them several times at less than fifty yards. Once while he was hunting with a double-barreled gun he let one of those lions come within fifteen yards, pulled the trigger, only to have the gun misfire. He was so upset he forgot all about having a second barrel. He—"

"Wait," I said. "Why didn't he put out some bait animals?"

"He did. Once he tied three goats to a heavy iron rail. The lion walked off with all three goats. Patterson shot at her but missed. He even tried strychnine on a dead pig, but found out that lions don't touch poisoned bait." Jones paused, listening. Our lion had gone. The oxen had quieted. Jones spat at a rock.

"Go on," I said. "What were Patterson's coolies doing all this time?"

"Oh, they panicked a couple of times. Once when the work train was coming in from Mombasa a bunch of them laid down on the track, and the train stopped to keep from killing them. Right away, about a thousand coolies leaped aboard with all their belongings. Fact is, one time all work stopped for three weeks because the coolies refused to budge from their tents. They'd dug holes in the floor—pits. They'd crawl in at night and pull logs over the top. But pretty soon the lions found food somewhere else and quit bothering the camp. So the coolies came out of their holes and started sleeping unprotected again. Then the man-eaters came back to live on coolie meat for a while.

"Sometimes Patterson had 'help' hunting them lions. Railway officials, police officers, even soldiers came to track down the killers. Some spent their nights roosting on scaffolds in trees, their guns handy. They did a lot of shooting but never hit anything. One fellow named Whiteside got off the train at Tsavo Station with a native sergeant named Abdullah. One of the lions greeted them by jumping on Whiteside's back, tearing nasty welts in it. She left Whiteside, knocked Abdullah down, and proceeded to eat him.

"Patterson spent a lot of time on tree platforms too. The lions, getting man-scent, used to circle the tree for hours, sniffing, grunting, and sighing. Lions always sigh when they're hungry. Sometimes Patterson would shoot and the lions would lope away up the railroad track to drag a coolie out of his tent for breakfast.

"Eight months went by before Patterson got the first man-eater. He shot her one night from his tree platform. The other man-eater went right along lunching on coolies for another month. But after polishing off the twenty-ninth coolie, one night she made the mistake of stopping under Patterson's tree to scratch herself. His slug finished her for good.

"Well, sir," Jones went on, "the coolies were so happy the lions were dead that they kissed Patterson's hands and feet and called him their savior. English newspapers got the story and made a hero out of Patterson."

"It just goes to show—" I began.

"Sure does," Jones said quickly. "Give Patterson a job building a railroad and you probably have a good man. But you can't get away from the fact that if he'd known the first thing about lions he'd have saved the lives of at least twenty-seven coolies."

My tracker, Ubusuku, a strapping, intelligent, coal-black Zulu, would have made short work of those man-eaters. Ubusuku's methods weren't sporting, perhaps, but he got results. One time shortly after World War I we were called off a job where we'd been using Mills bombs (grenades) to clear out a crocodile-infested pool on the Kasai River in the Congo and were told to go to a kraal near Kalonga in the Congo's southeast tip to get a man-eater that had sneaked a Kaffir woman out of her hut. Night after night, they told us, the lion had returned to the same hut to sniff about. The Kaffirs were crazy with fear.

I was pooped when we arrived late one afternoon, and went right to bed in the cleanest hut the chief could find. But not Ubusuku. He was after lion, and he didn't waste any time.

About three in the morning an explosion rocked the kraal. I ran out of my hut into a bedlam of shrieking, panicked Kaffirs. In a few minutes Ubusuku pushed his way through them and, grinning at me, announced:

"*Moonya, mabele, Simba pelele* [One, two, the lion is through]." Then, striking a pose, he said to the bug-eyed natives: "The lion, O Frightened Ones, has taken the long journey into the land of Fat Zebras."

The mob, hysterical with joy, carried him off to an orgy of beer drinking.

Ubusuku, who, contrary to orders, had brought two grenades with him, had tied a young pig in the hut from which the woman had been dragged. He waited downwind in darkness until the pig's frantic squeal told him the lion was in the hut, then sneaked up and tossed a Mills bomb through the door.

From time to time one hears of man-eaters doing in a white man. Investigation invariably shows the victim was careless beyond belief. After all, even a desperately hungry lion won't open a door or come down a chimney. He won't come close to a blazing fire. He won't attack from upwind, and he often warns of his preliminary approach by terrific roars. When he begins stalking, he grows quiet except for hunger sighs. In lion country, particularly when game is scarce, a man is just a plain fool to expose himself to attack. He doesn't have to.

People often ask me which is the least dangerous big game animal in Africa. Gorillas. If you want to make an old professional hunter mad, ask him if he

More than one hunter has learned, to his dismay, that there's no forehead under all that hair.

ever killed a gorilla. Most think that a man who'd kill a gorilla is a louse.

A gorilla has never been known to hurt a human unless the poor brute had been badgered or frightened beyond endurance. Gorillas live a family life that might well be emulated by humans. It's true that the gorilla's howl is nerve-shattering and that his habit of beating his chest, grimacing, and threatening an intruder is frightening. And when he tears up a small tree by the roots and lumbers toward you, banging his breast with one hand and threatening you with the tree in the other, few men can stand and call his bluff.

It *is* a bluff if you haven't pestered him, and if you stand, unmoving, he'll slow to a stop, tear the tree to pieces with his teeth, then turn away, grumbling and croaking at you over his shoulder. But if you wound him or return his threats, he'll crush you to a pulp against his chest.

Gorillas are protected against hunters by the governments now, but in old days these gigantic, peace-loving, lumbering vegetarians were murdered by the hundreds every year. Since their habits have become more understood, even museums are half ashamed to display their stuffed bodies. It's too much like displaying a stuffed grandfather.

One morning in 1922 in the Mount Karisimbi Forest, the very heart of Africa, I watched a gorilla family from the edge of a clearing. I was downwind, of course, and it was easy to hide in the heavy tangle of lianas, grass, brush, and branches. Beside me, Bob Schlick, an American cameraman, ground away silently. Two big black-haired males with silver-haired chests were pulling up roots and tubers and stuffing them in their mouths. Another male was eating young bamboo shoots. Two females slept in the sun, sitting up, back to back, their legs sticking out in front of them, their big bellies resting on their thighs. Four or five youngsters were rolling, wrestling, jumping, and frolicking all over the place.

After a while the largest of the males walked over and looked down at one of the females. In his hand he held a tuber. He reached out and pushed the female gently. She opened her mouth without opening her eyes. He pushed the tuber between her lips, then went back to his chums. The female, hands folded on her belly, eyes still shut, munched away contentedly and sleepily.

I watched a long time. Again the largest gorilla came back and looked down at his wife. Then he waddled over to a tree, sat down with his back against it, and after grunting something to the other males, folded his hands, closed his eyes, and slept.

That same year in the Cameroons, Schlick and I watched another gorilla family, two males, two females, a half grown male, and five or six youngsters of varying sizes. The Cameroon gorillas are smaller and have shorter hair than the ones we watched in the Congo. It may sound odd, but they seem unhappier.

Anyway, the sun was sinking toward the horizon and shadows were deepening among the trees. The two males kept looking from the sun to the children, from the children to the females, then back to the sun. The young ones scampered about in a sort of tag game. One of the males rumbled something to them, and they stopped as if shot. The other male got behind them and seemed to be shooing them toward a tree.

Suddenly the youngsters darted in all directions, throwing quick looks at the males. I swear they were laughing. It was apparently no laughing matter, though, for one male let out a howl that shook the forest. The two females leaped to their feet, and the youngsters went up the tree like a flash. As the half-grown male scrambled up the trunk, one of the females belted him a good one on the bottom.

The youngsters settled themselves in crotches of branches. The females climbed into trees on either side of them. They, too, settled themselves as the males watched. Then the males turned and looked long at the sun, beating their chests lightly, but making no noise. Finally they gathered up grass, twigs, and leaves, kicked them into a sort of bed, and lay down side by side.

I hope they slept well, for watching them filled me with a vague sadness.

LIONS

Just as there are many types of men, so there are many types of hunters and many types of hunting. Lion country, no matter in what part of Africa it may be, is pretty much the same: bush-dotted plains, sandy and rocky stretches with brush and reed-tangled growth along the rivers. Rifle work in lion country is a distinct art.

In bush-dotted plains, a lion standing and switching his tail seventy-five yards away seems to be almost two hundred yards from the gun. It takes long practice to judge ranges accurately, particularly if bushes line up for the shot as if one were looking down a street. Experienced hands estimate the apparent distance at half, then aim a little low.

On warm days when ground mirage (warm air) is running fast across the target, a bullet aimed directly at the animal at two hundred yards will sometimes miss by feet. You learn to compensate for ground mirage by aiming right or left, depending on which way the mirage is running.

What applies to ground mirage applies also to wind. I've seen cross winds that carried the bullet fifteen feet off target at five hundred yards. Usually, however, one has to allow just a few inches at two hundred yards.

Novices almost always overshoot downhill and undershoot uphill. At two hundred yards, with the sun shining, a .303 rifle-shot that should hit dead center will be high if a cloud passes over the sun as the shot goes off.

A rifle that shoots accurately in dry weather will shoot high in rainy weather; and practically every shot will miss if the trigger is pulled instead of squeezed.

Wounded and frightened, the lion is apt to charge. That's what the professional hunter expects and wants. There is just one rule for this situation—keep your head and shoot straight. Aim just below the tip of his nose. If the lion isn't badly hurt, don't waste time dodging—shoot again.

Many men, otherwise courageous, panic when a lion comes close. The things these men do are beyond belief. Once two Englishmen showed up at camp and hired me to help them find lions. They were eager for heads to hang in a clubhouse they were building.

They were fine-looking fellows. The elder, with a long, ragged mustache, was named Simmons. The younger man's name was Smythe. Ubusuku and I took them to lion country south of Okavarona in Damaraland. Both men were good on the veldt and easy to travel with on the desert. They shot well and brought down many a buck *en route*.

They were keen and fit when we spotted the first lion. It was late afternoon. The thornbushes were scattered. Almost everywhere you looked there were open spaces fifty or more feet across. We were talking about making camp when Ubusuku grunted and pointed to a low bush about one hundred yards straight ahead. Sure enough, there was what appeared to be a thick bunch of leaves at the bush top. I said:

"There's your lion. Peeking over the top of that bush."

"Where?"

I pointed and started to say we'd circle off at an angle to try to work closer, but without warning Simmons began shouting, "I see him!" and waved his rifle over his head.

"What the hell?" I said, and grabbed his shoulder. He jerked loose and, still yelling, began running toward the lion. I took a quick shot, and the beast's head disappeared. Simmons stopped, looking dazed and ashamed.

"Sorry," he said. "I got excited."

Ubusuku circled around behind the bush, then motioned us to come on. We found the lion on his back, kicking all four feet, growling, snarling, and spitting. I wanted Smythe to have the honor of killing him, so I motioned him to finish the job. Just as he raised his gun, the lion leaped up with a roar and charged straight at him. Smythe shot from the hip, missed, and the next instant was down, with the lion worrying his arm. I tried to get a fatal shot in, but Simmons jumped in front of me and started belaboring the lion over the back with the butt of his rifle. I stepped around Simmons, jabbed my rifle muzzle into the lion's ear, and pulled the trigger. The lion groaned and collapsed on top of Smythe.

Simmons, the picture of misery, stood muttering over and over: "I forgot to shoot. I forgot to shoot."

Smythe's arm, shoulder, and breast were badly mauled. We took him to the railway at Otavi, where his wounds were dressed. He recovered, not too much worse for the adventure.

A year later, in the Buganda country, two Frenchmen stood side by side when a wounded lion charged. One got cold feet and tried to run at the last minute. The brute, as lions always do, took after the man who was moving, knocked him ten feet with a swipe of a paw, then jumped on him and sank his teeth into a thigh.

The poor devil's companion, instead of using his gun, threw it aside and began pushing and pulling at the lion with bare hands. Both men were killed. Their gunbearer, a Swahili, picked up the discarded rifle, trailed the lion, and killed him. The head is on the wall of a saloon in Djibouti.

The most disgusted man I ever knew was a wealthy Swede named Hans Skaar. Skaar wrote me from Sweden and arranged to meet me in Nairobi. He said he had only a few days to spend in Africa; that all his life he'd dreamed of bagging a lion but had never been able to spare time for a hunting trip. Now he was coming to Nairobi on business and was going to take five days off. Would I help him get his lion?

Skaar was a grand fellow. We sat all one evening in a pub in Nairobi drinking whiskey and soda. He could talk of nothing but the lion he hoped to get. He was like a kid: asked a hundred questions, drank in tales

Alexander Lake 33

Ready to pounce!

Photo: Carol Resnick

of lion hunts until my voice wore out. The next morning he completed the business that had brought him to Kenya, and we set out in an old Ford jalopy, with Ubusuku and a shrunken, shriveled Wakamba boy named Tiete.

We abandoned the jalopy one day out and spent one full day among heavy thorns without seeing even a trace of lion. The next day about noon we came across a carcass of a Thompson's gazelle with the foreparts eaten. Lion spoor was thick about the spot.

"I think you'll get your lion," I told Skaar. "He's a male, too.

Skaar looked pleased. "I'd like a male," he said. "How do you know it's a male?"

"A male eats the foreparts of his kill," I told him. "Females eat the afterparts."

"Well," Skaar said wistfully, "it'll have to be today. I've got to leave for Nairobi at dawn."

He got his lion two hours later. The four of us had stopped to get a breather and to watch a herd of Burchell's zebras grazing in the distance. We'd long ago lost the lion's spoor, and hope of Skaar's achieving his ambition looked slim. As I stared into the distance I saw a movement from the corner of my eye. I turned toward it, motioning the others to stand still. I saw nothing.

I searched the plain with my eyes; searched it foot by foot. There wasn't a bush or a tree within a hundred yards—only tufts of dried grass and an occasional rock. I kept looking. Then I saw the movement again, and as if a picture were flashed on a screen fifty yards before us, I saw a male lion asleep on his side. A flick of the tip of his tail had given him away. Ubusuku and Tiete saw him when I did, but Skaar, although I pointed out the tuft of grass that grew by the lion's shoulder and the red rock close to his rump, never did see his lion alive.

It is not strange that an untrained eye cannot see so large a beast at times. I have stared for half an hour at a spot where Ubusuku saw a zebra, before the flick of an ear or the switch of a tail abruptly brought the whole animal into view. The lights and shadows, the contrast of dark bushes with yellow grass blend so perfectly with the dark and light stripes of the zebra's hide that the eye cannot distinguish its outline until movement gives it away.

Nor is it strange to find a lion sleeping alone in the open. There are no animals that a lion fears, and he'll sleep anywhere when his belly is full if he feels like having a nap.

At any rate, Skaar couldn't see the lion. I pointed out the grass tuft again and whispered:

"Shoot into that grass. Put your bullet right in its center. The way that fellow's lying, it should catch him in the back right between the shoulders. He won't be much good after that, and you'll have no trouble finishing him."

Skaar aimed carefully and fired. So far as I could see, the lion didn't even quiver. Skaar fired again, and this time we heard the bullet hit home. Still the lion didn't move.

We approached warily, guns ready. The lion was dead. Skaar's first shot, instead of striking the shoulders, had entered the back of the head, killing the lion instantly.

While Ubusuku and Tiete skinned the big fellow—he measured nine feet six inches from tip to tip and stood thirty-four inches high at the shoulder—Skaar sat dejectedly watching. He didn't speak until the boys rolled up the skin and we started on the back trail. Then he said, "Damn!"

As we parted at Nairobi, Skaar laughed suddenly. "You know," he said, "I've never seen a live lion." A funny look came over his face, and again he said: "Damn!"

Up to this point, almost all I've told about lions have been exceptional incidents. Actually, a steady diet of lion hunting is monotonous, and at times the professional hunter is hard put to it to keep his employer interested. Day after day goes by with almost the same routine. You spot some lions. You try to get close enough for a shot. The lions run away. You follow them. The lions either run again or disappear into heavy brush.

A man who has spent thousands of dollars equipping an outfit for hunting, and whose payroll for native and white help runs well over two hundred dollars a day, has to have results. If he wants lions, he wants lions. He can't be herded around the country too long without action or he'll fire you and get himself another professional.

When such a situation arises, we sometimes play a trick. It's a dirty trick, particularly on the lions. But it's one that's been played many times through the years.

We train a pride of lions to come out and get killed.

We had to do that for Herr Leonhardt Von Holtz,

a German whose home was in Austria. Von Holtz's "safari," as he loved to call it, had everything—guns, cameras, telescopes, tents, tables, chairs, sheets for the cots, canned goods by the ton, liquors, wines, books, electric and gas plants, kerosene heaters, Primus stoves, and blondes. He employed forty native bearers, and a body servant for each of his guests.

Two hunters, Jan du Toit and Lenny Gibson, Ubusuku and I met the caravan at Fort Johnston at the foot of Lake Nyasa. We trekked straight west across Northern Rhodesia for more than two hundred miles. We saw and shot klipspringers, reitbok, bushbuck, kudu, zebra, guinea fowl, steenbok, wildebeest, hyenas, jackals, one leopard, springbok, porcupines, a wart hog, and at least a score of baboons. It took a lot of game to keep that gang in fresh meat. Von Holtz and his friends were busy and happy at first, all dressed up in pink whipcord riding breeches, silk puttees, and English shooting jackets. His male guests were Hein, Vogel, Ranfurly, Bischoff, and Mertens.

Hein was a tough guy. He carried a blackthorn walking stick around camp and used it over the natives' backs. Everyone hated him. He was good with a rifle on small game, particularly at long range. He could really shoot.

Ranfurly was an Englishman, a good guy, but drunk most of the time. Vogel, Bischoff, and Mertens seemed regular. They had little to say. Von Holtz was the Prussian type, not a bad sort, but nasty with a drink in him.

We had bad luck with lions. We ran across a male

and female one morning and circled close. Von Holtz and Ranfurly took the shots. Ranfurly missed the lioness, but Von Holtz nicked the male. It roared like a bull crocodile, hunched itself up, and took off across the veldt, bucking and kicking. It kept throwing out its hind legs as if trying to shake something off.

The lioness outran the male about a hundred yards, then stopped and waited for him to catch up. Mertens, Bischoff, and Von Holtz blazed away at them, but overshot, and the animals loped away, the male still kicking out in that peculiar manner.

This went on for about half an hour. The lions would get behind a bush, and the female would look at us over the top. The hunters would fire, miss, and the animals would take off again at a slow gallop.

It began to get silly. Du Toit and Gibson dropped back in disgust. Finally I asked Von Holtz if he'd like me to bag the brutes. He cursed, so I dropped back too.

They gave up after a while and headed back to camp.

A few days later Ubusuku came in and said he'd found lion spoor on the far side of a steep-banked

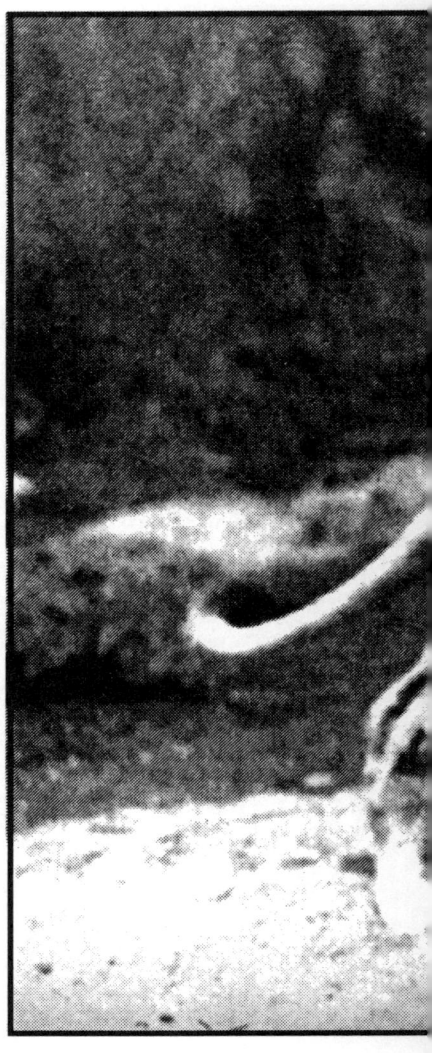

John Graudenz, 1924

The "King of Beasts" is not forgiving of a hunter's mistakes.

donga about five miles to the north. The gang left camp in good spirits. We took no natives with us except Ubusuku.

It was one of those days that come sometimes on the bushveld when mists hide everything more than a thousand yards away. Even for an old-timer, distances are hard to judge. A bush that seems almost out of rifle range will suddenly appear to jump toward you, and you learn that it is almost within throwing distance. On such days a four-hundred pound hartebeest racing across your vision at five hundred yards will sometimes appear to be the size of a forty-pound duiker.

Because there's no horizon, it's easy for a novice to become lost. Even old hands find themselves walking in circles, pausing once in a while with a feeling of apprehension. Being lost in the bushveld is one of the most nerve-shattering experiences a man can have. Years after, he'll dream of being lost and waken with sweat on his forehead, his hands damply cold, his heart thumping. I know.

That's why I warned everyone that morning to stay within sight of each other. But, having had twenty days' experience on the veldt, they thought they knew it all and were soon out of sight in all directions. I felt certain someone was going to get lost.

I sent Du Toit and Gibson back to camp to await developments at that end. Ubusuku and I sat down where we were to wait until our help was needed. Hours passed. The veldt was as silent as velvet. No rifle shots broke the stillness. No birds rasped and squawked in the bushes. Few birds on the bushveld have a sweet song. Usually, the more beautiful the feathers, the more unpleasant the voice. A secretary bird, great wings outspread, glided to a landing close by. He ruffled his feathers and, like a little old bookkeeper with a pen behind his ear and hands tucked behind him under the tails of a long coat, began pacing up and down as if in deep thought. He made a little hop, stooped over, picked up a short green snake with his beak, and flapped to the top of a thorn tree. Ubusuku slept.

I sat there staring absently at one of the tall clusters of grass that sometimes shoot up where antelope droppings have concentrated. This cluster, thirty-five yards away, was about three feet high. There was no wind, but I saw a shiver run up the grass as though a rat were nibbling at the roots. I looked beyond, where pinkish mists turned to purple in the distance. I thought of old Nicobar Jones and how, if he were sitting beside me, he'd be saying: "Purty. Purty."

Then it came to me that there'd been something unnatural about the shivering grass. I refocused my eyes on the cluster. Near its top, where it thinned out like a veil, I saw one unblinking yellow eye.

It was a lion, of course. I didn't want to shoot it and was about to waken Ubusuku so we could ease away. Then I thought of Von Holtz and figured he'd appreciate a head.

Slowly, a fraction of an inch a second, I raised my rifle toward my shoulder. My position was strained, but I didn't dare shift it. Muscles in the small of my back began to cramp as I looked quickly along the barrel and squeezed the trigger.

A lioness reared up on hind legs, pawed the air, fell over backward, and lay still. I expected Ubusuku to leap to his feet, but when I looked at him, he was grinning. I realized he had been lying there watching my performance all the time.

I shoved another cartridge into the chamber and walked cautiously forward. The lioness sighed deeply and died. Ubusuku skinned her. My bullet had got her an inch below that eye.

It was a cinch the lioness wasn't behind that cluster when Von Holtz and the others were about. In fact, Du Toit, I recalled, had been standing close to it just before he left for camp. She had been lying somewhere out on the veldt, and when Von Holtz and his guests blundered her way she had slipped behind them. Concentrating on the men who had startled her, she was no doubt as surprised as I when she peeked through the grass.

Ubusuku had hardly got the skin and head bundled when we heard what we'd been waiting for—rifle shots. Three shots close together—two shots well spaced—then three fired rapidly again.

S.O.S! Somewhere off to the west one **of** the hunters was lost and calling for help. Ubusuku replied with four shots, grunted in disgust, and headed westward at a run.

A half hour later I thought I heard shots far to the south but wasn't sure. For a long time there was only the silence. Then from far down an avenue of bushes I saw a man approaching. He came closer and closer, walking fast and looking neither to right nor left. He came straight toward me, and I saw it was Hein. His lips were moving. He looked at me without seeing me, eyes bleak.

I said: "Hein!"

He stopped in mid-stride, turned toward me, recognized me, and began to shake. I turned away to give him a chance to get his nerve back. Pretty soon he said: "I was lost."

"Yeah, I know."

He said nothing more until we arrived at camp. Then: "Thanks."

Ranfurly and Bischoff had found their way back to camp without trouble. Mertens had fired for help within a half mile of camp. Du Toit had gone out and brought him in. It was dark when Ubusuku showed up with Vogel. Von Holtz came in by himself a few minutes later. He was hopping mad. He strode to his tent without looking at us, and through the open flap we could see him pouring drinks from a square green bottle.

Ubusuku and one of the packers went out into the night to get the lion skin. When they returned I took it to Von Holtz's tent. He looked at the head for a moment, then cursed me in German. Told me to take the bloody thing out of his sight.

"I'll get my own lions," he said.

Next morning I handed Ubusuku a Galton whistle—a whistle too shrill for the human ear but easily heard by lions. Ubusuku knew what the whistle meant. He'd used it before. He flashed his teeth in a white smile.

"It comes to me, O *Baas,*" he rumbled, "that the hunters will have tales to tell to their grandchildren."

I told him to take Johannes, one of the camp boys, with him. I said: "When you find the lions, send Johannes back."

About a week later Johannes showed up as we were making camp. He'd seen our dust from the top of a *kopje* early in the afternoon. He told me he and Ubusuku had located a pride of several lions living among piled-up boulders seventy miles toward Mabombwe. "We fed them their first meal before I left," he said.

That is the trick. Feed a pride of lions until they get used to finding an antelope or a zebra at the same place every other day. Feed them until they quit hunting for themselves. As you throw down the bleeding carcass at the feeding spot, you blow the Galton whistle. The lions soon associate the sound of the whistle with food and come a-galloping.

For the next two weeks I worked the caravan slowly toward Mabombwe. We had two tries at lions, but no luck. Other game was plentiful, and Von Holtz got some good shooting in. I could see, however, that his failure to get a lion chafed his pride.

One afternoon we made camp within an hour of the spot where Ubusuku'd been feeding the lions. I sneaked off with Johannes to look at the setup. We found Ubusuku carrying away the bones of the animals he'd fed to the pride. The upended rocks were about two hundred yards from a flat-topped thorn tree. Behind the rocks, gray-green brush straggled off in a ragged line. Ubusuku had picked a feeding spot where the tree was between it and the rocks. He said there were three females, two males, and two young cubs. They didn't sleep among the rocks, but behind them, in the brush. They came through the rocks to the feeding place.

Next morning at dawn I started out with Von

Holtz, Hein, Ranfurly, and their gunbearers to hunt for meat. Vogel, Mertens, and Bischoff had hangovers and wouldn't get out of bed. Gibson stayed in camp. Within an hour we climbed out of a donga and walked right into a herd of springbok. The animals took off, jumping high. Five were bagged before the herd bounded out of range.

Just before noon I steered the party toward the thorn tree. As we approached I saw Ubusuku coming to meet us. He was pausing, kneeling, getting up, walking a few yards, squatting, and getting up again, as if following a difficult spoor. His act was so natural that no one could have guessed he knew we were there and watching all the time.

We stopped under the thorn tree, watching the big Zulu approach. Finally he indicated that he saw us, and held his hand up over his head, palm forward. That was his signal to me that the lions were all in their lair. I signaled: "Go ahead." He stepped behind a bush and blew the Galton whistle.

As the first lion, a male, walked slowly out from the rocks, I said:

"Two hundred yards, twelve o'clock, one finger right—lion!"

As Von Holtz and the others whirled to face the rocks, the rest of the lions came into the open. They milled about for a few seconds, then one of the males put his mouth to the ground and let loose with a halfhearted roar. The other male switched his tail impatiently. One of the females started toward the feeding place at an easy lope. The others followed. As the thorn tree where we stood was between them and the expected food, it appeared that the whole pride was charging us.

I couldn't help admiring the reactions of the three men. Ranfurly said: "My aunt!" and thumbed the safety catch on his rifle. Hein whipped his gun toward his shoulder. The butt caught in his bandoleer, and he cursed softly. Von Holtz laid his cheek against his rifle butt and waited. The gunbearers took off toward Ubusuku in a bounding group.

Von Holtz fired at about one hundred twenty-five yards and dropped the leading lion. Two quick shots, and he bowled over the next one in line. Hein wounded one of the females. She turned back with a roar. Hein fired at her again, and she did an about-face, made a few jumps, then stopped and bit at her side. Three shots exploded, and she keeled over. That left a male and a female, and although they were hit several times, they kept coming. When they got within about sixty yards, I thought it time to take a hand, but even as I raised my rifle, both dropped, rolling, kicking, and snarling. Von Holtz walked up and put a bullet into each.

He reloaded his magazine without a word. Then he put an arm across my shoulders and said: "It has been a good day."

I watched the Kaffirs start to skin the beasts, and felt like a heel. The two little cubs whined beside the body of their mother. I walked over and picked them up.

ELEPHANTS

IF YOU know elephants' habits and temperament, if you work with a good tracker, use caution, and keep your nerve, you're in little danger from the big beasts. A lion, under some conditions, might attack without provocation. It's possible that a leopard might leap from a tree on an unsuspecting man; but it's a cinch that no elephant will attack you unless you've done something to fill him with fear or fury.

Many persons have been killed by elephants; many have been injured; but in every case I've known or heard of, the tragedy was the fault of the victim. Carelessness, ignorance, and unreasonable fear are the killers.

The first man I saw killed by an elephant was a Boer prospector, Willy de Beer. I was meat hunter for Nicobar Jones at the time, and De Beer joined our transport wagon outfit so he'd have protection on the long, difficult climb over the Mount Elgon hump from Kitale on the Kenya side to Mbale just inside Uganda.

The second day out, and several miles in advance of

the wagons, Jones, De Beer, Ubusuku, myself and five Swahili carriers entered a clearing thickly dotted with acacia, butter, and dwarfed thorn trees. Thinking we might scare up an antelope or two, we spread out and began a stalk from bush to bush and tree to tree.

Suddenly, dead ahead from behind a heavy fringe of brush came the shriek of an elephant, followed by shrill trumpetings from other scattered ones. Each man ducked behind the nearest bush or tree as five heavily running brutes—four adults and a half-grown bull—loomed through the branches less than sixty yards away. Something on the other side of the clearing had stampeded them.

They came too fast for us to do anything but crouch and wait in breathless suspense. They came thundering, heads bobbing, tusks high, dodging obstacles. Each of us knew that if he stayed put behind his fragile blind the herd would probably dodge past, leaving him unharmed. Not once in a hundred charges will an elephant crash through a tree or shrub. But there is always that one chance.

De Beer would have been perfectly safe where he was, for he had taken cover behind a clump of three ragged-topped stumps. But as the line of shrieking elephants bore down on us, De Beer's nerve broke. He dashed from his cover, running straight across their path. One of the cows hit him with her foreleg. He had popped in front of her so abruptly that I doubt she ever saw him. At any rate, he somersaulted under the young bull.

The frightened herd kept right on going.

We buried De Beer that night, wrapped in a new red blanket.

Alexander Lake

The elephant, up close and personal.

The tales the Big Game Association hunters tell in the pubs of Nairobi are little concerned with the long, hot monotony of spooring or the humdrum of routine elephant killing. They're mostly tales of tragedy and near tragedy in which every elephant is a monster and every monster is a killer.

These are tales for innocents.

Except for an occasional old rogue, male elephants are the first to flee from a hunter. Females get between the males and danger, and push and hurry them into dense brush out of harm's way. And the males usually keep right on going, leaving females and youngsters to get out of trouble the best way they can.

It is the females who have courage to face peril. It is pregnant cows who attack with little warning. Always, an old cow bosses the herd. Only once in a while is a rogue nasty, but a pregnant cow is always mean. The sight or scent of a hunter is often all the provocation she needs for attack.

Yes, elephants sometimes attack, but except for a bypassed "sneaker," they give plenty of warning. I've never known an elephant to charge without first drawing back his ears in an odd quarter cock. This does not always mean he's going to try to run you down, but it does mean he's going to do *something*. He may turn away, charge to the right or left, or he may come straight at you.

Men have died because they believed that, in charging, an elephant always comes with ears full-cocked, trunk up, and trumpeting. They often do, but sometimes they come with trunk down, tip curled back, and without even a preliminary grunt.

When this happens, the elephant isn't fooling.

The sudden appearance of a man within a few yards of an elephant doesn't frighten or anger the elephant so long as the elephant doesn't get the man's scent. Usually on such a downwind appearance the elephant shows curiosity only. It will probably fan its ears full and stare at the intruder with a puzzled expression in its mild eyes. Sometimes it will turn and walk away, only to stop within a few yards, come back, and have another look.

If the hunter moves or makes a noise, the beast sometimes makes short, blind side rushes or starts a bluffing charge, trumpeting as it comes. If the hunter stands his ground, chances are that the elephant will turn aside and stride toward the herd; which, warned by its blasts, bunches together and moves off, emitting short roars and angry rumblings.

When a man is winded *but not seen,* the herd searches for the point of danger with extended trunks. When the direction of the threat is located, all members of the herd turn to face it, then turn and shamble away, heads bobbing, babies squealing as they try to hide under mothers' bellies.

It is questionable if in bright sunlight an elephant can recognize a man at more than twenty yards. At dusk and at early dawn he sees a little better, but at forty yards he can't tell a man from a stump. And elephants don't charge stumps.

Elephant noises give a professional hunter a pretty good idea of the mood of an individual or a herd. Purring noises in the throat mean contentment. Males often purr when approaching their mates. Low, squeaking noises indicate pleasure. Loud, continuous rumbling from the throat means apprehension. The same sound, pitched lower, is made by a wounded elephant. Shrieks by cows may be warnings to totos (babies), preliminaries to an attack, cries of alarm, or a threat. Calves make coughing sounds when talking to their mothers. Adults cough when irritated.

When hit by a bullet, an elephant gives a roar. Sometimes he roars when angry. Elephants' guts rumble at short intervals day and night. They dung every forty-five minutes, which makes it easy for trackers to know how far ahead the herd is. They spend much time flapping their ears against their withers. The noisy chewing of leaves, twigs, and bark never ceases except when the herd is dozing during the heat of day.

Most white hunters know and recognize these noises, but to black trackers like Ubusuku the sounds have significance which white men never perceive. For instance, Ubusuku would point to an elephant and say:

"That one's belly is filled with pains. He will soon wander off by himself. He will be easy to stalk because he thinks only of his guts."

Or he might say: "That young bull wants that fat cow. The fat cow is the wife of the bull with the rough skin. The old bull knows what is in the mind of the young bull. Soon they will fight."

Or: "That old one gasps for water. He is about to die. He will go and squat in the water of the river. But the water will not bring back his years. He will die in the water. The crocodiles will eat his flesh, and we can get his tusks without trouble."

And almost always Ubusuku would be right.

Elephant hunting isn't all it's cracked up to be. Big game is interesting, but hunting it entails hard work. Danger? Not much to a man who knows what he's doing. But even the best get careless.

One late afternoon in September near the Tanganyika-Kenya border, about forty miles east of Lake Victoria, Ubusuku and I stood in heavy brush listening to muffled noises from a herd of elephants we'd trailed for five sun-cursed days.

I was tired, sweaty, thorn-gouged, and miserably wondering why I didn't get a less exhausting and more profitable job than hunting, when Ubusuku suddenly reached down, grabbed up two handfuls of moist elephant dung, and splashed it on my back and chest.

A bull elephant bathes in the Zambezi River in northern Zimbabwe (1990) during a Resnick photo safari.

"*Gashle, Baas,*" he said under his breath. "The wind changed. Maybe they smell you."

It was an old Pygmy trick—rubbing a man with dung so elephants wouldn't get his scent. Elephants invariably become agitated when they smell a white man and frequently lumber away in panic. Often when they pass a spot where a white man has stood, they stamp on it viciously.

Ubusuku loosened his hold on me, rubbed his polluted palms on his bare calves, stepped to a tree, pinched off a piece of decayed bark, ground it between his palms, and let the resulting powder trickle to the ground. Sure enough, the breeze which a few moments before had been blowing from the elephants to us was now blowing from us to them.

I forgave him the dung.

The job we were on now was a toughy. I had an order from a billiard-ball manufacturer for yellow ivory, and he wanted it in a hurry. Elephant herds in East Africa had been hunted so persistently that they seldom left the shelter of dense brush until dusk and always returned to their coverts toward dawn.

It would have been a much easier job had the manufacturer ordered "blue" ivory from the less skittish elephant herds of the wet areas of the Congo. But for billiard balls, only East African ivory with its yellow tinge would do. It was coarse-grained and had "spring" to it.

We had picked up the spoor of a small herd and followed it across plains, down an endless ravine, over brush-grown slopes, through knee-high grass sopping with dew in early mornings and crackling with dryness in the afternoons. We crawled on hands and knees through heavy thornbrush and stumbled over boulder-strewn flats. The elephants had adopted the "long stride," which meant they were migrating to some spot Lord knew how far away.

Nevertheless, we gained on them, for manure droppings were fresher each day. Today, just before sunset, we again entered heavy brush. Broken branches and fresh dung scattered about had shown the herd had browsed there just a short time before.

We moved slowly, Ubusuku testing the breeze every minute or two. Sometimes he stuck his tongue out as if tasting the air. Again he let powdered bark fall from his hands. Sometimes he just sniffed. We kept downwind, moving without a sound. Abruptly Ubusuku stood erect and turned his head from side to side, listening.

At last he grinned, his teeth a white flash in the shadows, and pointed ahead, a little to our left. I cupped my ear with my hand and heard the short, coughing sound of a calf talking to its mother and imagined I could hear the rumbling of an elephant's guts.

It was at that moment that Ubusuku had plastered me with the gobs of dung.

By the time Ubusuku, armed as always with only a stabbing spear and his hand ax, returned from scouting the elephants, I'd become used to the smell of the manure. I followed the big Zulu into the brush. It became an almost impenetrable jungle.

Stooping, creeping, sometimes wriggling on my belly, keeping my rifle clear of snags and branches, feeling cautiously with hands and knees for dry sticks that might be buried under leaves and grass, I marveled at how effortlessly elephants push their way through tangled growth, leaving little evidence of their passage. I marveled also at the strange drive that makes a man hunt ivory for a living when he could get a comparatively easy job digging ditches or something.

There's no tougher hunting in the world than elephants. That is, physically. It's heat, cold, rain, flies, ticks, ants, sweat, open plain, and dense forest for days on end without ever sighting a herd.

To a novice, a charging elephant seems like approaching doom. An old hand knows that at least half the time a charging elephant is bluffing and that if the man holds his ground the beast will stop uncertainly, make little rushes here and there, and finally lumber away. When this happens within thirty or forty yards of the gun, the hunter often has a chance to get in the deadly shoulder shot. Because of the mass of blood vessels and nerves in the shoulder muscle, two or three shots placed there will kill the elephant with shock before he can move fifty feet.

On the other hand, when the elephant keeps on coming, trunk up and mouth wide open, the hunter can place a soft-nosed bullet smack into the back of the animal's mouth, step quickly aside, and watch the elephant crash forward and skid to a crumpled stop.

Sounds heroic, but it isn't. At from fifteen to

twenty yards that mouth shot never fails if placed right. Camera hunters frequently make photographs of charging beasts from ten yards. A hundred misadventures can happen, of course, because elephants don't always obey the rules, but there's just one situation that promises the hunter the near certainty of a squashy, tusk-punctured death. That is to become so intent on the animal ahead of him that he fails to hear a killer elephant coming on him from behind. It's happened many times; an unseen elephant bypassed in the tangled growth, the hunter's single-minded concentration on the animal in front of him, the uncannily silent approach of the bypassed beast, and his sudden screaming charge from behind. I've known only two hunters to come out of such a predicament alive. Both men were horribly mangled.

Nine times out of ten, elephants do the thing you expect them to do. That tenth time's the one where only your wits, your speed, and damn-fool luck keep you from being killed or crippled.

I didn't know it, of course, but as Ubusuku and I stalked this particular herd, that tenth evil chance was about to happen—and if it hadn't been for Ubusuku and his American hand ax, I'd have been just another victim—a victim of my own carelessness.

The dense jungle thinned abruptly, and from behind a screen of branches we looked out upon a park-like clearing. Through the fringe of brush, shadowy shapes of three elephant cows loomed against the evening sky. Two of them, about seventy-five yards away, stood broadside to us. The third one faced us, her head showing above a bush about fifty yards straight ahead. She was making squeaking noises of contentment and flapping her big ears listlessly against her withers. From the far end of the clearing came noises of mothers and their totos squealing and coughing.

It was obvious that the herd had no hint of our presence, but Ubusuku, fearing a switch in air currents, kept testing the wind continuously. The cow nearest had the largest tusks, far larger than the average of thirty to forty pounds. I estimated they'd run about seventy pounds each—140 pounds for the pair.

She was standing just right for a forehead shot, or, as old hunters call it, a "duffer's" shot. The top part of an elephant's head contains nothing but air cells. Bullets placed there bother the animal very little—so little that a beast will sometimes take two or three shots there and walk away—or charge—depending upon its mood. Furthermore, an African elephant's forehead is convex, and a bullet is just as apt to ricochet as not. The forehead shot can get a man into a lot of trouble.

I wanted to get close to the bush over which the big cow was dreaming, but that required crossing twenty-five yards of open glade. To distract the elephant's attention, Ubusuku slipped away like a soundless black mamba, and I waited for him to get the animal looking his way.

An elephant always faces the direction of suspected danger and must turn its whole body to do so. That's what happened now. Ubusuku shook a small tree. The cow lifted her ears to half cock and turned awkwardly to face the sound. She wasn't alarmed, however, and slowly heaved herself back to the original position.

Short as the distraction was, it enabled me to wriggle to within fifteen yards of the bush. I figured the elephant stood about the same distance beyond it. This placed her thirty yards from me. By the time she resumed staring over the top of that single bush, I was flat in the grass.

Then she saw me. Her ears cocked full. Her eyes bugged. She took one or two steps forward, stopped, stared hard. Then an air current must have eddied so she could smell me. She pulled her ears back in a peculiar quarter-cocked manner that usually precedes a charge, instantly fanned them out full again, curled her trunk up, raised her tusks, screamed, and came at me.

I was sure she'd duck around the bush, for even the angriest charging elephant dodges stumps and obstacles in its path. Because she was screaming, I thought she was probably bluffing. I figured if her charge was just a threat she'd stop close to that bush.

She dodged around the bush all right. But she wasn't bluffing. She came right on. I wasn't too worried. This was a case for split-second timing. I'd been through it before. I was lying prone, holding my rifle with my right hand at the point of balance. Now I flipped the barrel upward and pressed the toe of the butt against the ground to lever myself into a kneeling position. My hand was sweaty. It slipped from the smooth wood. The rifle slapped flat against the ground, with me, off bal-

This Tanzanian gentleman is carrying about 80 pounds a tusk.

ance, sprawling on top of it. No chance for a shot now, just barely time to scramble out of the way. I scrambled. My foot caught in the rifle sling and I fell on my face. I rolled to one side just as the beast reached the spot where I'd been. She stopped, puzzled, made a short rush to one side, swung back, saw the rifle, and stamped on it angrily. Before I could make a break for it the cow saw me, straddled me, and started to kneel. Somehow I twisted so that, while directly under her, my feet were toward her head.

From this point things were blurry. I remember seeing her right hind leg towering like an immense pillar above me. Through some freak arrangement of the trees of the forest I was able to look at the setting sun as through a hole. I thought: *It's far, far away.* Then, crouching behind the cow was Ubusuku, a sort of miraculous visitation. I saw the flash of his hand ax as it severed the tendons of the elephant's left back leg about a foot above the ground. I saw that foot tip up on edge, its sole vertical to the ground. It seemed to have broken off at the ankle. It was a centuries-old native trick—this tendon-severing. Most animals, particularly a rhino, can get along fine on three legs, but the elephant needs four. With a disabled leg, an elephant has no more fight in him.

Ubusuku dragged me out and threw me clear. He pulled me erect. We ran for the edge of the clearing. We stood hidden in the scrub and watched the elephant. From her throat came a deep rumbling, but her trunk hung limp, her ears drooped, and she stood as still as a statue. She was finished and she knew it. I felt sorry for her.

I turned toward the rest of the herd just in time to see the last of them push into the bush at the far end of the clearing. They weren't panicked, but they were making a noise like muffled drums.

My rifle was under the disabled cow. My second rifle was miles back at last night's camping place with our porters and gear. All I had in the way of a firearm was an old worn-out .45 Colt in a holster strapped to my leg. I used it occasionally to put wounded game out of misery. I sneaked along the elephant's left side, from behind. She knew I was there but didn't even try to turn her head; just lifted her ears slightly and deepened her rumbling. I reached the .45 high and shot her through the temple. She didn't even quiver. I put the next shot through her eye. She collapsed, stretched her trunk straight out along the ground, and died.

She measured ten feet seven inches at the shoulder. Her feet were almost sixty inches in circumference. Spread out, her ears measured eight feet seven inches across the forehead.

As we chopped out the seven-foot tusks, Ubusuku said not a word, but I could tell from the way he snorted and grunted that he was disgusted with me; humiliated to be working for a hunter so careless that his life had to be saved by his tracker. After the tusks were laid side by side he said:

"The fish whose head gets too heavy swims with his behind out of the water, O Baas."

I said: "My foot caught in the sling."

"An ape caught with his hand in a gourd blames his bad luck, O American, but the trapper knows that the ape is a fool."

I said: "Thanks."

"My behind was not out of the water," he said.

An ivory hunter is not necessarily a slayer of elephants. Much of the commercial ivory comes from hippo teeth and wild boar tusks; and in my case, about seventeen per cent came from collections of tusks made by Pygmies and other natives.

There is little money in honest ivory hunting these days, although the price is about as high as it has ever been—at least fifteen shillings a pound. But elephant licenses are costly, and expenses for trackers, food, transportation, and other safari items are away out of sight.

India is the big market for ivory. Most elephants are slaughtered illegally by natives with poisoned arrows. The elephant "bootleggers" are organized and controlled by Tanganyika Indians, and their ill-gotten loot is smuggled out of the country by Arabs.

There's no such thing as an elephant graveyard, popular belief to the contrary. When elephants feel death approaching, they seek water. They submerge themselves in river pools and swamps, letting the waters cool their last fevered moments. After death their bones are stripped of flesh by crocodiles and fish. In time the sands and mud of river or swamp bury the skeletons—tusks and all.

Natives prospect these swamp and river bottoms and over the years pile up quantities of tusks. An ivory hunter who can persuade owners of such collections to sell or trade them to him usually gets a bargain.

Once from a Pygmy tribe in the Ituri Forest country in the Congo I got 5,200 pounds of ivory for giving a little chief named Bobo the eyelashes of an elephant I'd just shot. Those eyelashes were the greatest thing that ever happened to Bobo. He believed their possession would give him magic powers and that he'd become as fertile as a rock rabbit.

When my porters moved in to get the 131 tusks, the tribe threatened us with poisoned darts, but Bobo, displaying his little package of eyelashes, quelled them easily. As we pulled out with our hoard of "teeth," Bobo climbed on a fallen log, pounded his brown chest in imitation of a gorilla, and with his belly button protruding like an oversized walnut screeched:

"I will be the father of thousands. I will breed like a hyrax."

Maybe he was well paid for the ivory, after all.

There's a mystery connected with that find of ivory. About half the tusks were the brownish-black-barked, tight-grained ivory of West Africa; the other half, the straw-colored bark of East African tusks, and there'd never been any East

African herds closer than five hundred miles to the cache.

The logical explanation is that those teeth were loot from Arab caravans probably massacred years before.

The hunting of hippos for their teeth is now considered about as low as hunting lions with hounds. It just isn't done by decent white men any more. Hippos are such mild, inoffensive brutes and give up so easily when cornered that hunting them is almost like shooting cows in a pasture.

I'll never forget the morning my trackers surrounded a big male hippo that had wandered outside the fringe of reeds along a small river in Uganda. When the beast saw he was cut off from the water, he sat down on his haunches and stared at me, looking exactly like a big pig. I didn't have the heart to shoot him, so I drove a bullet into the ground close to his rear end.

He got up, looked at me reproachfully, and lumbered off about one hundred feet, then sat down again. His mate, hearing the shot, came waddling out of the reeds, saw her husband, walked over to him, and lay down beside him. He stretched out with his head on her belly and went to sleep. I walked away in disgust.

I've bought, or wangled, thousands of hippo teeth from natives, who usually kill the big animals by harpooning them exactly as whales are harpooned; that is, by driving a spear into them, a spear with one end of a rope tied to it, the other end fastened to a heavy rock. The wounded beast, unable to drag his painful burden long, drowns.

BABOONS

IF A MAN wants to test his hunting ability I suggest that he try chacma baboons. No animal, not even the African buffalo, ever led me such a futile chase as did those gray rascals. To this day I'm not sure that I have more brains than a baboon.

During most of 1911 and 1912 I was a meat hunter for a wagon transport outfit plying between Salisbury in Rhodesia, and Congo, Tanganyika, and Kenya points. My pay was about one hundred dollars a month and I supplied my own guns and ammunition. I had just about given up hope of saving enough money to buy my own wagons and oxen when word came that the Transvaal Government was offering a bounty of five shillings a tail for Magaliesberg District baboons.

As there were an estimated eighteen thousand baboons on a thirty-five-mile strip of the Magaliesberg Range, I had visions of quick, big money. Old-timers told me I couldn't make a living shooting baboons, but I knew better. Hadn't I seen plenty of baboons in the tree country of Rhodesia and Tanganyika? They hadn't acted very smart to me. They knew enough to climb down out of the trees and hide in the long grass when white men came along, and so far as I knew, that was about the extent of their cleverness. I'd never had occasion to shoot one.

What I didn't know was that baboons that have never been hunted are one thing, but baboons that have been under rifle fire are something else. And those Magaliesberg baboons had been hunted plenty.

There had been two years of drought, and the baboons along those hills were hungry. From being eaters of berries, grains, wild fruits, and insects, they'd become eaters of meat. Not only were they playing hell with farmers' crops in the foothills, but they were killing and eating pigs, sheep, lambs, goats, chickens, and even dogs. They were an economic menace that had to be stopped. Hence the five shilling bounty.

It should be kept in mind that these big, ugly, dog-faced, four-handed brutes weighed up to 130 pounds, and that no animal can adapt itself to changing environment as quickly as they. They're cunning, controlled by leaders, have phenomenal eyesight, are emotionally unstable, and two of them can, when driven by frenzy, tear even a leopard to pieces.

Well, I set out to make a stake hunting baboons. After all these years, I still feel like a fool when I think of it.

There were three hundred baboons in the troop

I began stalking on a Magaliesberg *kopje* one morning as they came out of their sleeping place at dawn. I stalked these baboons all during a day so hot that the rocks of the *kopje's* slopes were heated like stoves. For hours there were always baboons in sight, but never once did I get closer than one thousand yards to one. Every move I made was watched by baboon sentries posted on high rocks or in scrub trees. Whenever they thought I was getting within rifle range of any of the troop, those sentries would cut loose with a roaring "waugh" of warning and my quarry scampered to safety.

As the day advanced, those baboons began making a game of it. Sometimes young males would turn their buttocks toward me, and through binoculars I could see them making faces at me from between their legs. Once I passed close to a high outcropping, and baboons on top of it hurled stones, sticks, and dirt down on me and beat it before I could get a shot at them. The troop shouted, roared, grunted, and shrieked all day long. They knew the range of a rifle and kept just far enough away to make shooting useless.

By late afternoon my feet hurt. The bandoleer of .303 cartridges over my shoulder had chafed the side of my neck raw. It was time to go back to the hut at the mouth of the *kloof,* but I wanted a breather, so I sat on the edge of the *krans*, my feet dangling in space, and lighted a sweat-soaked cigarette.

The rose-copper sun settled toward the top of the opposite *kopje*. Below, in the rocky, wooded canyon, shadows lay purple among the tree ferns and wild date trees. To the north, the bushveld stretched to the distant ridge of the Swartbergen, and all the plain between was hazy with lavender and silver mists.

The *kopje* on which I sat—in fact, the whole Magaliesberg Range—was a series of red-brown rocky hills dotted with *stamfrachte* bushes and thorn trees. Every *kopje* was the home of at least one troop of baboons, and in the *kloofs* between the *kopjes* lived tiger cats, leopards, antelope, snakes, and lizards.

I put out my cigarette, leaned my chin on the palms of my hands, and rested my elbows on my knees. About twenty feet directly below me was the wide-spreading top of a *moepel* tree. The cliff wall against which my heels rested dropped sheer to the bottom of the *kloof.* My rifle lay beside me, close to my right hand. I closed my eyes to listen to the silver tinkle of the little stream down there among the shadows.

Behind me I heard the barely audible clatter of a rolling pebble. I turned my head. An old baboon, mouth open, fangs gleaming, hands outstretched, was within inches of grabbing me by the head. Behind him I caught a quick glimpse of a score or more of his silent fellows. I jerked forward, kicked at the cliffside with my heels, and launched myself into space. As I fell I turned in the air until I was falling backward. Falling, too, was the baboon—struggling and twisting frantically. My sudden dive had upset his calculations, and his rush had carried him over the cliff.

We crashed through the tree branches together. I bumped and thudded from limb to limb and stopped at last, hanging with my belly across a branch. I don't know what happened to the baboon, for by the time I'd grunted my way to the ground he'd disappeared. But above me the ugly, dog-like, grimacing faces of his pals leered at me from the edge of the cliff. It took an hour of roundabout climbing to retrieve my rifle. By that time the baboons had returned to their sleeping place.

If that baboon had got his hands on me, he and his pals would have torn me to pieces. When one of those fighting males grabs a man or a dog, he gets hold with all four hands, throws himself on his side, and rips chunks out of his victim with his teeth. I once saw four baboons drop on a leopard from an overhanging rock. One got between the leopard's forelegs and sank his fangs into the throat. Another got between the hind legs and sank his teeth into the soft belly. The other two tore chunks of meat out of the leopard's sides not only with their teeth, but also with their hands. In little more than a minute the leopard was practically stripped of flesh. The baboon that had gripped the animal's throat staggered away from the body of the victim, sat down a little way off, and looked down at his cascading bowels, ripped from his belly by the leopard's claws. The other three baboons, seemingly unhurt, tried to pull him erect by his arms, but he died as they lifted him. They let him fall back and for several minutes sat beside him, mumbling and talking to one another. Then they dragged his body to the brink of a small dry ravine and pushed it over the edge. Baboons always push their dead over a cliff.

What made the attack on the leopard even more grisly were the hoarse shouts and roars of the rest of the troop as they watched the massacre from the nearby slopes. When they saw that the leopard was dead, the roars and shouts turned into screams and shrieks of joy, for they had witnessed the death of their most terrible enemy. The leopard kills more baboons than all human hunters put together.

It isn't often that baboons get an opportunity to attack a leopard. He's a silent, cunning, deadly hunter. He lurks atop a rock or hides among the leaves of a tree, sometimes for hours, waiting for a baboon to wander away from the troop. Then the leopard stalks him and leaps upon him like a streak of yellow light. He sinks his fangs into the small of the baboon's back, paralyzing him, and in almost the same movement disappears into a hiding place. There he lurks until darkness, then goes back and carries off his kill. When members of the troop see such an attack, their cries are a heart-rending combination of terror, hatred, sorrow, and hopelessness.

When I crawled out of my pup tent at the foot of the *kopje* the second morning, the sky above the hill was a solid sheet of golden copper that changed swiftly to a faded blue. Baboons shouted and barked all over the upper half of the slope. The turmoil was continuous. Young baboons raced, wrestled, and tumbled. The older baboons roared and bellowed and squawked, apparently for the sheer hell of it. I was so eager to be after them that I only half warmed the pan of stale coffee on the Primus stove, gulped it, picked up my rifle, and began what I thought was a careful stalk. But I hadn't gone a hundred feet up the grade before the tumult and the shouting died, and a vast silence took its place. I peeked carefully over the top of a rock. There wasn't a baboon in sight.

I kept on climbing, slipping from rock to rock, crawling across open spots on hands and knees, ducking behind occasional ridges, and from time to time pausing to search the slope above me. No baboons.

After about half an hour of this I happened to look behind me and saw a black, long-snouted head peering at me from around the edge of a rock about twenty-five yards back. I swung to get a shot, but the head disappeared. I felt silly. I'd been behind that very rock myself two minutes before.

I sat down, placed my elbows on my knees, and trained my rifle muzzle where the head had been. No soap. I saw a flicker of movement to my right from the corner of my eye, whirled, and saw two heads leering at me over the top of a dwarfed castor-oil bush. Both heads disappeared instantly.

Remembering the attack on me the afternoon before, I jumped to my feet and looked at the edge of the rock above my head. Nothing there. I pulled back the rifle bolt to check the cartridge in the chamber, saw it was all right, shoved the bolt home, looked up, and saw a full-grown baboon sitting upright, staring at me, fifty feet away. I shot with the gun across my belly. The bullet struck at the animal's feet and ricocheted harmlessly with a smacking snarl.

With the sound of the shot the *kopje* became a pandemonium. From behind rocks all around me dark forms raced shrieking, bellowing, and barking up the hill. I'd been literally surrounded. While I thought I was stalking them, the whole damned troop had been stalking me.

I got in five shots as the mob scattered upward. Four times I heard the thud of a bullet hitting flesh. One shot missed. Four baboons were dead when I got to them. Four tails. Twenty bob! About five dollars. But it was many long weeks before I got four baboons in one day again. It was nine days before I got my next one.

Probably the biggest difficulty in learning to hunt baboons is that you never know what they will do next. You think you have their habits figured and find to your chagrin that they seem to have changed overnight.

Next to man, there are greater variations in bodily measurements and facial characteristics among baboons than in any other animal species. It isn't long before a hunter learns to distinguish individuals, and if you stick around a troop long enough you can learn to identify every beast in it.

During the next nine days I learned to recognize quite a few of the old gray devils. Their sentries were always perched in trees or atop rocks in full view but never less than one thousand yards away. No matter how patiently I lay hidden, no matter how carefully I sneaked up on some wanderer, those damned sentries would spot me and shout a warning. After hours of fruitless ambushes and stalks that failed, I'd lie on my belly and study the sentries through my field glasses. One big fellow seemed to be all teeth. I named him "Teddy Roosevelt." Another reminded me of a goat, for some reason. I called him "Billy." Another I called "Snoopy." Another, "Simple Simon."

One morning as I lay well hidden in some dried grass behind a *stamfrachte* bush, an old fellow wandered down the *kopje* slope and sat down in the shade of a flat-topped boulder and stared out over the valley. It was Teddy Roosevelt. I judged the distance was seventy-five yards. I was on my belly and I stopped breathing as I slowly snuggled the rifle butt into my shoulder. I got the fore sight way down in the bottom of the V sight, lined it on the side of his head, and started my trigger squeeze. Something moved on the boulder above him, and I held the shot to look. Three tiny black heads were poked over the edge of the rock, looking down at the old fellow—three baby baboons about the size of spaniel pups.

Something in the old boy's attitude told me that he knew the youngsters were there. I lowered my rifle to watch. The three leaped together, landing on the old fellow's shoulders and back. He collapsed with a roaring squawk that could have been heard for a mile. The babies scrambled all over him, biting, tearing at him, roughing him up with all their puny strength. He pretended to fight back, rolling over and over, making prodigious snaps at them with his powerful jaws, pushing and mauling them with sham ferocity.

Finally the old gentleman lay motionless, apparently dead. The three little rascals strutted stiff-legged around him, fantastically cocky over their victory. Then they scurried behind the boulder and appeared on top of it again. The old baboon sat up as before, looking into the distance. Again the three leaped. Again the big male collapsed with a roar of simulated terror. Again the youngsters overcame him after a battle.

This went on until the old fellow wearied of the game. He brought it to an end by picking one of the babies up by the neck and smacking his bottom. The three disappeared like a flash. Once more the old devil sat down to contemplate the veldt stretched out below. I couldn't shoot an old character like that in cold blood. I stood up and let him see me. He leaped to his feet, threatening me with short, deep-throated barks from wide-open jaws. With his tail in a stiff inverted U, he backed around the boulder and was gone.

A few days later a Colonel Capel of the Transvaal Signal Corps showed up at camp accompanied by a Zulu tracker he called "Schelem." Capel was making some sort of survey for the Army and asked me if I could show him an easy trail over the *kopje*.

I told him there was a trail that skirted the Crocodile River where it poured through a gorge at the eastern foot of the hill. This trail was a narrow ledge along the cliff face. It ended abruptly after half a mile at a point where a large section of the cliff had fallen into the gorge. At this break it was necessary to climb down over a great pile of upended rocks and detritus resulting from the slide. After about fifty yards of this, the ledge, still narrow, continued unbroken to the other side of the kopje.

Capel was red-faced and fat. His neck bulged over the collar of his military tunic, which he insisted on wearing despite the hot sun. Schelem was black, young, and powerful. I decided to go with them as far as the break in the trail.

We were in the middle of the pile of rock debris when with a ferocious roar a large male baboon shot out from behind a boulder and faced us where the trail ledge began again. The brute was in a rage, and every time he cut loose with a roar his head jerked forward. He seemed to be about to tumble from his position, so eager was he to get at us.

His first bellow had hardly left his throat when baboons sprang into view on a hundred rocks. They howled, shrieked, barked, and roared, all the while moving closer to us with short, threatening rushes. Capel threw up his rifle, but Schelem knocked up the barrel.

"If you shoot, *Baas,* we are dead men," he said.

"He's right," I told Capel. "Those baboons are hysterical. They might tear us to shreds."

Capel's face grew almost purple with anger. He shook a fist at the baboon on the ledge and said: "Damn your impudence!"

The troop kept moving closer, a step at a time. Their din was so great that I had to shout. I said: "I've heard about this sort of thing. There's nothing we can do but remain quiet." Schelem tapped my shoulder and pointed behind us. A group of seven or eight males barked and roared about fifty feet away. The largest moved toward us slowly.

It was touch and go. A few fast shots might panic the mob, but, on the other hand, might bring them down upon us. I noticed that the members of the main troop were shifting their positions. The females' babies and young baboons moved back a little. The males moved into the van. It was formation for an attack.

I said: "Let's sit down."

We sat.

The baboon on the ledge was less than twenty-five feet from us. The hair on his shoulders stood up like that of an angry dog. I looked straight into his eyes. They were yellow. They were so filled with hatred that I continued to stare into them in a sort of awe. Suddenly his eyes shifted from mine, and a roar died in his throat. He seemed to stare over my shoulder. His eyes kept flashing back to mine for an instant, then away again. Finally he backed up a couple of feet, cut loose with three roaring barks, and slipped quickly behind a rock.

Those barks must have been a signal, for the whole troop turned and ran. They kept on going until they were just little moving spots far up on a high shoulder of the kopje.

Schelem wiped his forehead with the heel of his hand. He said: "In my boyhood this happened. A white man shot too soon. He was killed. It is all right to shoot them now, *Baas*."

I shook my head, but Capel emptied his magazine at the retreating troop. It was silly, because they were far out of range.

I said good-bye to Capel and watched him and Schelem climb onto the trail and plod out of sight. Then I sat down again to let the shaking die out of my legs.

Although I didn't get another baboon for nine days after those first four I had bagged, I did get a leopard. I sold his hide later for five pounds. I had been stalking three young baboons who were so interested in scorpions under the rocks that they forgot to be cautious. I managed to get within a hundred yards of them and was edging to one side in an attempt to get two of them in the line of fire, hoping the same bullet would do them both in. They, however, slipped away when a sentry barked a warning.

I was hot and sweaty. My knees were as sore as boils from sharp stones. I had thorns in the palms of my hands and ants kicking around on my skin just above where the belt went around my waist. I was cursing in vexation when I noticed that the *kopje* was strangely quiet and that the whole troop of baboons was racing toward the hilltop in complete silence.

Near the top they rallied. They gathered in a bunch, spread themselves out in a semicircular line, and started back down the slope. The line wheeled, faced a heavy thicket of brush, and cut loose with a threatening uproar that reverberated from all sides. With mouths wide open, heads jerking forward with quick thrusts, the baboons approached the thicket, their shoutings mounting in hysteria but their pace slowing foot by foot.

Then I saw the leopard as he slunk, belly to the

ground, out of the other side of the thicket. For an instant I debated whether to try a shot at him or at the baboons. I chose the leopard. I flipped my back sight to a notch over two hundred yards, and as he slithered over the edge of the *krans* I let drive.

He screamed and went over the cliff. It was the first time I'd heard a leopard yell in agony, and I'll never forget it. I found blood on the brink of the cliff. Uncertainly I searched the *kloof* below. I knew that a wounded leopard is a far more dangerous beast than a wounded lion, and I didn't relish facing one—not down there in the semi-gloom of the heavily wooded ravine.

I figured his den was probably in some cave on the wall of the *krans* far up near the *kopje* top. To trail him I'd have to follow the bed of the brush-overgrown stream, push my way through tangles of exposed tree roots, climb around a score of little waterfalls—all in heavy shadows.

The cliff was low at the point where the leopard had gone over. About twelve feet down, to a bed of ferns. I decided to hang by my hands and drop into the ferns, hoping there were no sharp rocks hidden beneath them. I got to my knees and looked over the edge for a landing spot.

Almost directly below me was the leopard. He lay on the ferns in a patch of mottled sunlight. He was looking up at me, his shoulders half raised, his hind legs out to one side. His mouth was wide open. When he saw I'd spotted him, he began snarling with quick liftings of his upper lip. He started making threatening passes at me, first with one forepaw, then the other.

I shot him smack between the eyes. He laid his head on his right paw, very gently, and seemed to sleep. I shot again, aiming at the side of his head. The head bumped off the paw; the tail lifted slightly, then fell limp.

When I finally got up enough nerve to drop down beside him and had satisfied myself that he was dead, I saw that my first shot had broken his back just above the hips, but to this day I get weak when I think of what might have happened to me had I dropped down that cliff without looking.

Young baboons are playful, but constant attacks by leopards, pythons, and man make most grown baboons brooding and touchy. Sudden noises set them to roaring and screaming. The invasion of their *kopje* by anything that might be an enemy often throws the whole troop into screeching, barking hysteria. At such times the leaders, too, seem unable to resist the emotional storm

I witnessed one of these mass attacks of hysteria one afternoon when a python looped down from a limb of a tree in the *kloof* and wrapped his coils around a young female baboon. Her screams brought the whole troop to the edge of the *krans*, where they went completely crazy. They roared, screeched, milled about, ran off in all directions, returned to the edge of the *krans* to look down on the tragedy being enacted below, jumped up and down with bared fangs, screamed and barked, then ran off, only to return and go through the whole procedure again. The leaders were almost as hysterical as their charges.

I wanted to get close enough to shoot the snake's

squawking victim to put it out of its agony, but every time I edged toward a position from which to shoot, the raging troop made awkward, howling jumps in my direction. Finally I took a chance with a long shot—a steeply downhill shot, made almost impossible by the violently threshing battle. I must have hit the python somewhere, for he lost his tail hold in the tree, and snake and baboon began cartwheeling all over the place. The python banged away with his nose at the baboon's face. The baboon jerked her head from side to side and finally succeeded in getting her fangs into the python's neck. All the while the snake's tail was whipping about, searching for something to wrap around for a purchase. Without that tail hold, it was impossible for the python to crush the baboon's life out.

At last the end of the tail flipped around the base of a small bush, and with a final despairing squawk the baboon died. For a moment the python, still coiled around his victim, was still, and I pumped four or five fast shots at him. He began uncoiling slowly, with strange, sudden jerks. He wriggled clear of the dead baboon and threshed about with the upper half of his body. His lower half didn't move.

The troop of baboons, silent now, lined up along the edge of the *krans*, staring down. Abruptly they began howling and screeching again, then stampeded to the top of the *kopje* and disappeared.

I scrambled down into the *kloof*. The python, his guts protruding from two bullet holes near the center of his body, was helpless. His back seemed to be broken. I placed the muzzle of my rifle close to a staring eye and pulled the trigger. His head jerked to one side and a ripple of relaxation ran down his body. I cut off the baboon's tail and left the two of them there; the baboon lying as if asleep, with blood oozing from the corner of her mouth; the snake with just the tip of his tail twitching feebly.

It finally dawned on me that I was going to starve to death if I depended on stalking by myself to accumulate baboon tails. I could see I was going to get few close-up shots. Most of my killing would have to be done at ranges from four hundred to more than a thousand yards. So I spent three or four days lying in a blind behind a low, flat rock from which grew two *stamfrachte* bushes, taking ranging shots at trees, boulders, and outcroppings all over the hillside.

That's how I got my first sentry. His usual post was in a dead *moepel* tree from which I'd seen bark fly with a ranging shot at 840 yards. This fellow used to sit in a crotch, his back against the trunk, keeping his eyes peeled for approaching trouble. He usually spotted me a few minutes after I left the pup tent in the mornings, and his warning "waugh" kept the troop out of range.

However, this morning I had gone to my ambush while the troop was still in the sleeping place. I set my sights, got well under cover, made sure I was down-wind, and waited. The sentry crawled to his usual perch just at dawn, and as the sun lifted over the *kopje* his body stood out in strong, black silhouette. I figured he was about six feet above the spot where the bark had spurted from my ranging shot, so I raised the back sight one notch and drew a bead on his belly. I squeezed the trigger. He threw up one arm, slid off his branch, clutched feebly at the tree trunk, and disappeared from sight at the bottom of the tree.

As usual when a shot was fired, the whole troop set up a raucous screaming. When the baboons spotted me stumbling up the hillside to get my victim, they rushed over the top of the hill and disappeared on its other side.

My ranging shot had been accurate to a foot. My bullet got him ten inches above where I'd aimed. A pretty shot, and no doubt I'd get several sentries in exactly the same way. I was mistaken. Never again while I hunted that *kopje* did a baboon perch in that tree.

That afternoon I got a three-quarter-grown male at four hundred yards. I was sitting, sweating and scratching in my blind, when I saw him climb up and sit down on a boulder. I don't know what he was doing there. The rest of the troop were far away.

That's the way it went. Some days, one baboon. Other days, two or three, but all the time the shots got longer and longer, and I missed a lot. I decided I'd have to have someone circle the troop and drive them toward my ambush, so I got Charlie, my young M'shangaan camp boy.

Here's the way I explained my plan to him: "You, Charlie, will chase the baboons around the *kopje*. I will lie behind cover, and when the baboons pass points of which I know the exact range, I'll blast away at them."

Charlie liked the idea. He knew that all baboons hate Kaffirs. But he had a special grudge against them. One time a tame baboon in the Parktown Zoo in Johannesburg had urinated in his drinking cup, and when Charlie came close the old joker had thrown the mess in Charlie's face.

Well, my idea didn't work out. For days I lay beside my rock waiting for baboons to wander close to one of the spots I had selected. Charlie was like a baboon himself and, instead of tending to business, kept sneaking away to pick *stamfrachte* apples and wild berries.

Then one midday two leaders showed up suddenly on top of a rock I knew to be exactly 278 yards away.

I turned over on my stomach, took up a solid prone position, and was about to open on the two when I noticed they were crouching to attack something on the other side of their rock. I squeezed the trigger. One baboon collapsed and lay still. The other, roaring savagely, sprang at whatever he saw below him.

It was Charlie.

He screamed in terror, but the scream choked off abruptly. It probably took me thirty seconds to scramble to Charlie's aid. The baboon—the one I called "Snoopy"—was on his side, all four hands holding Charlie, his teeth sunk in the boy's upper arm. Charlie seemed to be unconscious. Snoopy saw me, screeched hoarsely, and got to his feet. I let him have it through the head.

I knelt down by the young Kaffir, but before I could even touch him, the baboon I'd thought dead atop the rock leaped upon my back, knocked me heels over head, and at the same time ripped my forearm open from wrist to elbow with one of his fangs.

I remember seeing my bared forearm muscles sticking out like the picture of a skinned arm in a doctor's book. At the same instant I noticed that the baboon, reaching for me again, had had the top of his head blown off just above his eyebrows by my first shot.

There wasn't time to shoot, although miraculously I was still holding my rifle near the end of the barrel. I swung it like a club. The baboon crumpled. It was then I noticed I'd been using my ripped arm as if it were uninjured.

Charlie and I were a bloody mess. I wiped Charlie partially clean with my shirt, saw that he had a badly mauled shoulder and that one of the baboon's fangs had gone completely through his left hand. Apparently Charlie had shoved his hand into the baboon's mouth in an effort to keep his own throat from being torn out.

He sat up as I examined him. He must have been out of his head, for he kept repeating in M'shangaan: "I have no bowels. I cannot be cut in two."

We walked ten miles to the farm of an Australian named Ross. He hitched up a Cape cart and took us to the hospital in Pretoria.

When able to hunt again, I found I didn't want to kill baboons any more. Something about them had got under my skin. They're not human, but they sometimes seemed mighty close to it. Ugly, fascinating devils! I made up my mind that someday I'd study them as a friend—not as a hunter.

5
RHINOS

Rhinos have given me more bad moments—and more laughs—than all other big-game animals together. They're nervous, fretful, itchy, dim-witted creatures with extraordinary hearing, a keen sense of smell, and eyesight so poor that they can see but a few yards beyond their front horns; and half the time those horns interfere with what little vision they do have.

To the average sportsman-hunter, a charging rhino appears to be a thundering demon. To the average professional hunter, a charging rhino is just a big, dull-witted brute making a fool of himself.

I know the viewpoint of the greenhorn, for I've acted as support gun for all kinds—from sadistic blood-spillers to regular guys who know what trophies they want and go after them as sportsmen should.

There are only three reasons for getting killed by a rhino or by any big game—ignorance of their habits, carelessness, or plain foolishness.

I know one old professional hunter who boasts

that he's been tossed three times by a rhino. A greenhorn could be tossed once without losing face. After all, he's got to learn. A professional could be tossed once and be credited with a mental lapse. But to be tossed *three* times proves a man more stupid than a rhino.

Tossed by a rhino! Sounds pretty deadly. Yet five out of ten who are tossed get up and walk away. Four require considerable doctoring. The tenth man takes off for the Happy Hunting Grounds.

It's different when they trample you.

One of my first professional encounters with a rhino ended in the death of a man. Mario Galli was an animal buyer for a game contractor. He brought me an order for two live baby rhinos for the Jardin des Plantes zoo in Paris. Ubusuku and I went to the Uaso Nyiro country in northern Kenya after them. Galli had a yen to get himself a rhino and came along. He wasn't the easiest man in the world to hunt with. He was touchy and hot-tempered. At first he refused to let me watch him try out with his .303, but when I told him I'd act as guide for no man until I knew how he could shoot, he consented.

I set up a battered eight-inch pot lid at one hundred paces. Galli missed it offhand. He missed it kneeling. He missed it sitting, elbows on knees. He missed it prone. I took his rifle, got the front sight into the back V until it made a perfect W and let the shot off at six o'clock. The bullet went through the lid one inch above dead center. It had been nicely zeroed for two hundred yards.

I adjusted his sights for one hundred yards and

worked with him for two hours. He got so he could put his shots into the lid from a prone position. Standing, he was hopeless. I said: "Ordinarily I wouldn't guide a man who shoots so poorly as you do. But if you'll promise not to shoot unless your rhino is in short grass so you can lie down to it, and if you'll take no shots unless the beast is broadside to you so you can aim at a spot halfway between the base of his ear and his eye—okay."

He promised.

I said: "Remember, you're shooting a .303 with a 215-grain bullet, so if you're going to drop him, you've got to hit him smack in the temple."

"You don't have to draw a map," Galli said.

I was pretty green myself at that time or I'd have seen we were destined for trouble and would have sent Galli about his business. Instead we left the Model T Ford flatbed at Archer's Post and headed upriver.

One morning about eight o'clock as we climbed out of the dry river bed, there was Galli's rhino under a clump of dome palms in short grass about seventy yards out from heavy brush. He'd been wallowing in a river pool and was covered with red mud.

Rhinos are easy to stalk in the open from downwind. They can't see you coming, and you can get within yards of them. Chances are their tick birds won't bother to squawk if you move up slowly and noiselessly. I've often had a rhino spot me before his birds did. It's all in moving cautiously and placing your feet carefully. Grass clumps sometimes hide dry sticks. Might as well shoot off a pistol as to step on one. Don't kick pebbles. Might as well throw stones.

Galli was pretty good on the stalk but was nervous and kept swallowing. When we were fifty yards from the big fellow, I motioned Galli to lie down. He took a good position, laid his face along the rifle butt—and coughed. The rhino lifted his head. His birds rose in a startled flurry. The rhino's ears flipped erect. He raised his snout and sniffed, then started toward us at a hesitating trot. Galli fired, hitting the beast in the flank. The rhino turned with a wheeling snort and broke for the bush. I didn't want him to get away, for I would have to trail him. Can't leave a pain-maddened beast at large to kill some unsuspecting devil.

I had about six seconds to get in a shot before the brute would disappear into brush—and the only target I had was his backside. I was about to try to place two fast ones on his back knees, but Galli fired from behind me. The rhino slowed to a trot, circled as if bewildered, then, turning toward the brush, broke into a snorting gallop. For a moment as he wheeled I had a chance at the side of his head, but Galli, yelling and waving his arms, jumped in front of my gun. Before I knew what was happening, he had galloped after the rhino, and the two of them were swallowed in a tangle of dwarf thorns.

Ubusuku, who had been standing behind us like a big black statue, jerked the American hand ax he carried from its holster and bounded after Galli. I ran along the edge of the bush looking for an opening that might lead into a clearing. No soap.

I heard the rhino snorting and crashing about; heard Ubusuku yell a warning; heard Galli shoot.

It took me a couple of minutes to break through to where Galli was lying. He was dead. Not tossed. Stepped on.

That's hot country up there east of Archer's Post. Next to the Danakil country of northern Ethiopia, it's the hottest territory this side of hell. This particular area happened also to be ant country. We wanted to bury Galli right then, but the ants had already gotten to him—millions of them. We left them to finish their job and went after the rhino.

There was blood here and there shoulder-high on the brush on the left side of the trail he'd made as he banged his way through the thorns. That was from Galli's first shot. There was blood on the right-hand bushes, about three feet from the ground. There was blood, lots of it, in a pile of fresh dung.

Ubusuki said: "He is shot through the bowels, *O Baas*. Even now he is thinking of dying. He wants to lie down. We will find him on his side. There will be no fight in him."

The big Zulu was almost right. We came upon the poor beast two hours later. He was sitting, forelegs braced, his head hung low. I put the muzzle of my rifle in his ear and squeezed the trigger. His front legs collapsed and he lay face down in a monstrous, crumpled bundle.

Ubusuku chopped a circular gash in the skin around the horns, tore the skin loose, and lifted it off—horns and all.

We camped on the red sands of the river bed that night beside a hot, salty pool. In the morning the ants were gone from Galli and we buried his fresh white bones. We marked the grave with slabs of lava rock, then went after our two baby rhinos.

Galli's death makes a messy story and sheds no credit on me. If I'd been a licensed hunter of today, I'd have lost my license permanently. Everything I did was wrong. Galli couldn't shoot. He was nervous and erratic. I took up a position that permitted him to jump in front of my gun when he went berserk. I should have killed the rhino when Galli's first shot didn't drop him. The episode has all three characteristics of a big-game fatality—ignorance, carelessness, and damn foolishness.

The rhino is normally timid and easily flurried. He's intensely curious. On the plain when he sees something strange, like a man, his curiosity and timidity combine to make him uncertain, nervous, defiant, and flustered. He first gazes in astonishment. Then his eyes twinkle; his ears flip forward; his tail comes up. He starts toward the object at a trot. He stops. Stares. Trots forward again. Stops. Tilts his head from side to side to get the front horn out of his line of vision. He trots closer, finally stopping within a few yards. Up to this point he usually can be turned aside with shouts and waving arms.

Usually when he turns away he breaks momentarily into a gallop but slows again to his cocky trotting. Sometimes he trots in a circle and comes back for another look. Ordinarily, however, he keeps on going.

If he decides to charge, he breaks into a gallop. He can do thirty miles an hour, but as a rule his charges are at a twenty-mile-an-hour clip. He comes snorting. Nine times out of ten a shot in the foreparts or the head will send him wheeling away, and he isn't likely to stop until he's well out of range. About as often as not he changes direction in the midst of a charge and goes thundering off at an angle. If, however, he determines to carry his charge through, he lowers his head for the thrust at about twenty yards. From that moment he is blind; can see only the ground in front of him. Anyone who isn't dead on his feet can step aside and watch the big chump flounder past.

If a bush happens to be in his line of charge, the rhino sometimes rips into it, snorting like a grampus. Then, thinking he's eliminated his enemy, he trots off, tail up, ears perked, every movement of his body expressing fatuous self-satisfaction. He makes you think of a weak-minded baseball player trotting to the bench after unexpectedly batting out a home run.

Don't kid yourself that you can hit a big-game beast just anywhere with a .600 Nitro-Express and drop him cold every time. It's true that many support gunners use a .375 Magnum or a .475 High Velocity bullet when backing up a sportsman-hunter. But don't think for a moment that they just blaze away. They place the heavy-caliber slugs just as carefully as I'd place a .303—preferably in the temple.

More rhinos are dropped in their tracks by a well-placed .303, .38/.56, 8m/m, or a .348 than are ever dropped by a .450, .475, or .600. A thousand times more big game is killed with rifles costing less than $200 than with rifles costing more than $400.

There's little point in arguing about rifle calibers. If a man's convinced he needs a .600, you aren't going to argue him into switching to a .220. There's a psychological need in some men for a heavy shooting iron. A novice should have all the confidence he can muster. Some men feel "naked" with a small-caliber rifle in front of an elephant.

At least ten of Africa's best-known big-game hunters, however, preferred a .256 for all game. Those hunters are Buxton, Hodson, Littledale, Loder, Lyell, Millias, Selous, Stigand, Sheldon, and Vanderbyl. W. D. M. Bell, professional elephant hunter, usually used either a .275 or a .256 for bagging the big tuskers.

Personally, I prefer a military Lee-Enfield .303. If deprived of my .303 I'd be perfectly happy with a 6.5-mm. Mannlicher-Schoenauer and a 160-grain bullet; with a .270 Winchester and a 150-grained soft-nosed bullet; or, for that matter, I'd be satisfied with any good modern rifle of comparable size.

I once acted as guide for five "sportsmen" who hailed from California. They'd stopped in England and picked up rifles costing in the neighborhood of $1500 apiece. Smallest caliber they had was .450. One day in the Congo they poured fourteen .450 slugs into an old cow elephant. She barged off, bellowing and shrieking. She ran almost a half mile before she collapsed.

Two shots in the muscles of either shoulder would have killed her almost instantly from shock.

All five men swore they were shooting at a shoulder. To make the story more disgusting, the cow was a *poenskop,* without tusks.

It isn't how hard you hit them; it's *where* you hit them.

A rhino will run a hundred feet with a .450 through his heart. He may live for hours with a .600 through his guts. He'll travel miles at a good clip with one leg practically shot off.

On the other hand, a .303 through an eye, ear, or through the temple will drop him in mid-stride. Three .303s in the shoulder muscle will kill him before he's gone twenty-five yards. The bullets smash the concentration of big nerves and blood vessels in the shoulder, and the shock kills within two or three seconds.

I have no quarrel with heavy-caliber guns if a man can handle them. Few men can. No use shooting at game with face puckered up and both eyes closed. It happens that although I hunted Africa from end to end I never found a spot where I needed a big-caliber rifle. If I couldn't have placed a .303 in the temple of a rhino barging past within ten yards, I'd have quit hunting.

One time I took a Frenchman named Villeneuve out after rhino. He was a reasonably good man with a rifle; didn't mind finding lizards and scorpions in his boots in the morning, nor spiders dropping from tree branches into his coffee. He did a good job on antelope, zebra, and giraffe. But every time a rhino came galloping toward him he'd lose his nerve and either throw down his gun and run, or stand frozen, leaving me to turn the brute.

One night back in camp I cranked up the Ford flat-bed, called Villeneuve out into the veldt, and, yelling at him to run, took after him with the truck. He stood in ludicrous unbelief as the truck lumbered down on him, but when he saw I really meant to run over him if he didn't get out of the way, he jumped. I made a skidding turn and came roaring back at him. He dodged clear, and I heard angry curses as I jolted past him. I circled wide and came at him again. This time he ran, keeping ahead of me for a short distance. But he tired quickly and I closed on him. He stopped and faced me, a rock in his hand. I hadn't seen him pick it up. When I was within a few feet of him, he let that rock go. It missed my head by inches.

When I stopped the truck and grinned down at him, he sputtered so hard he couldn't talk. I've never seen an angrier Frenchman. When I explained that if he could evade a Ford at twenty miles an hour he could certainly keep away from a charging rhino, his face lighted and he clapped his hands. Suddenly he threw his arms around me and kissed me on both ears. I said: "You even had time to pick up a stone, dodge me, and throw the stone. Why can't you side-step a rhino traveling at only twenty miles an hour and as he passes stick your muzzle in his ear?"

"Ha!" he said, and tried to kiss me again.

Villeneuve evaded the next charging rhino like a dancing master and put his bullet smack under the beast's rear horn—the perfect spot for an instantaneous kill.

Rhinos that live in brush or haunt the high-grass

areas are no different in temperament and habits than rhinos of the plains. But hunting them is something else. The same rule holds good, however, that a man killed by one has displayed carelessness, ignorance, or foolishness.

A man who goes alone to stalk rhinos in high grass is either simple or has a suicide complex. It's safe enough hunting them if you place your trackers in trees to overlook the terrain and spot the big beasts as they shoulder through the grass. Sometimes a grass rhino will charge on getting a man's scent. But your scent is widely diffused, and the best the rhino can do by smell alone is to barrel in your general direction. Two thirds of the time he'll charge off at right angles to you, anyway.

If he's heading for you and you don't feel like sticking around, beat it if you can push through the grass. If you get away safely, give yourself a talking to and see if you can't persuade yourself to stay out of high rhino grass in the future.

The biggest danger from rhinos in the brush is in getting into a spot where the bush is so heavy you can't dodge a charge. This won't happen if you send your trackers ahead to smell out the touchy animals. The chances are that the mere smell of your trackers will be enough to send the rhinos lurching toward safety. Should a brute be feeling like a scrap, your natives can warn you in time for you to choose a clear spot for the encounter—or to climb a tree. But remember, if you climb a wait-a-bit thorn, you'll be about as bad off as if you'd let the rhino get you. Those thorns are like a million tiny swords.

The place to get bush and grass rhinos is at the water hole. Rhinos feed every hour of the day except during their midday siesta. They'll travel a long way to water, sometimes fifteen miles, and prefer hitting the water holes at dusk or during the night. However, if their skin folds are full of ticks and biting bugs, they'll head for the water holes at any time, day or night. They drink, then wallow in the mud, smothering their insects and filling their armor cracks with cool, healing slime.

Don't get between a rhino and the water if he's thirsty. That's the only time, except when wounded, that the brute will actually be savage. They stand for no interference with their drinking and will attack anything—elephants, lions, buffalo, oxen, or man.

In the brush, the moment the rhino gets suspicious, he stands concealed, motionless and alert. Sometimes he'll stand for an hour, his head up, his only movements the twitching of his ears and the turning of his head from side to side as he "feels out" the air. When his legs get tired, he sits down, forelegs straight, and goes on with his sniffing and listening. When his suspense gets too great, he lurches away. He'll attack only when noises and smells get him so puzzled and nervous that he explodes into panic. Ordinarily, a charging rhino is a frightened rhino.

No matter how clearly you think you hear the rustling wings of death as a rhino thunders down upon you, *keep cool and shoot straight*—and you'll get out of it. Remember that a shot will always turn him and that a wounded rhino, once turned, will seldom come back.

I realize that a sportsman facing his rhino for the first time isn't going to jerk a book of rules from his pocket and start reading. I know that when he sees a ton and a half of prehistoric dynamite bearing down on him at twelve yards a second he's going to wish he were back home reading about the whole thing in a magazine.

It's a terrific experience in his life and he's going to see it that way as long as he lives. You'll never convince him that the rhino wasn't angry but was in a panic. Anyway, he can't see that it makes any difference what spiritual or psychological mood the snorting, thundering beast was in.

Well, he blasts away. The brute turns. The sportsman lets fly at the side of its head. The beast goes to its knees. Another shot, right behind the eye. The rhino topples on its side. That's fifteen seconds of powerful excitement! What if he *could* have waltzed to one side and let the brute barge past? He didn't. He stood up to it. He's a sportsman.

He'll forget that an old hand was standing by, looking along deadly accurate sights every second—just in case. But what's the difference? He *thought* he was at death's door. So far as his emotions are concerned, he had the narrowest squeak of his life. He faced it—and won. And he's got a head with a twenty-five-inch horn to prove it.

Silly as it sounds, if a bullet hits the tip of the rhino's front horn, he'll go down—knocked out—for about six seconds.

That horn rests on his skull in such a way as to prevent heavy, violent shocks *from the front* from jarring his brain. But it doesn't protect that brain from shocks that are hard and *sharp*. Furthermore, if you were to give a rhino's horn a hefty bang *from the back* with, say, a baseball bat, he'd go out like a light—momentarily.

Why do people shoot rhinos? Sportsmen kill them for trophies. Natives kill them for food—and there's no tastier ham in the world than rhino ham. I killed rhinos to fill orders from taxidermists in Pretoria, Johannesburg, London, and Berlin. What do taxidermists want with rhino heads? Trophies for sportsmen; the same sportsmen who, when skunked on a fishing trip, stop at a market and buy a catch to take home.

There's a big, profitable market for the horns too. East Indians buy them, powder them, boil the powder in wine, and sell the concoction as an aphrodisiac. Rhino hides are used for sandal soles, native shields, camel buckets, and anything else that must stand up under hard usage.

But the most valued part of the rhino is the penis. From it is made the *sjambok,* the most vicious whip in the world. It's a slender, tapering whip, as pliable as whalebone, as tough as steel. One cut lays the flesh of a man open to the bone. I'd as soon shoot a man as to hit him with a *sjambok.*

Some *sjamboks* (also called *kibokos)* are made from the hide of the hippo, rhino, or giraffe. But the most brutal, the most desired, are the *sjamboks* made from the stretched and sun-dried rhino penis. Prussian and Belgian army officers in Africa delighted in them.

To make a *sjambok,* a flatiron or any two- or three-pound weight is tied to the small end of the penis. The "meat" is hung in the sunlight from the big end. It stretches from day to day, growing more slender all the time. When thoroughly dried, trimmed, oiled, and polished, it's as sleek and deadly as a three-foot green mamba. A lighter but just as savage *sjambok* is made from the penis of an ordinary bull.

Stupid is the word for rhino. In certain seasons the males fight each other sometimes for hours. One always dies. They snort, puff, blow, and crash about in the brush, slashing one another with their horns. Finally one gets his horn up into his opponent's guts and pulls and tugs to get it out. Sometimes the vanquished collapses on the victor with the horn still buried. Then the winner wrestles and pushes until he turns the dead one over. He stands looking at the corpse, steps back a few paces, and gives it another two or three bangs with his horn.

One moonlit night I witnessed a battle royal among five rhinos, each gashing, slashing, and puncturing the nearest to him. On and on went the struggle. One was dead by the end of the first hour; three at the end of the second; the remaining pair continued the uproarious duel for another two hours. Then they withdrew and stood making whining snorts, gathering strength to go on. Abruptly one collapsed. The other turned and wandered into the brush. When I approached the corpses, I saw that every square foot of the body of the last one to die was gashed, gored, and bleeding.

Next to humans, I think the rhino is the least "civilized" of the animals.

Before I forget, I want to mention the "white" rhino. He's gray, of course. He's not the "white" rhino, but the *weit* rhino, pronounced *wite*. It's a Dutch word meaning *wide* and refers to his wide, square nose. He's larger, slower, and dumber than the black rhino. His neck is longer and he can really plow a furrow in the ground. Where the black rhino is a simpleton, the "white" one is completely *non compos mentis*. That's why he's practically extinct. He's so nearly extinct that a live one today is worth from $20,000 to $30,000. I don't know where to tell you to look for one. Perhaps up along the Kenya-Ethiopia-Somaliland border.

If you like baby pigs, you'll like baby rhinos. While the mother watches fondly—and I mean fondly—the little rascals slide on their bellies in the dust, chase leaves blown by the wind, and run squealing after wind-blown feathers and blades of grass. Male rhinos are not permitted near the little ones. However, when the babies are grown, the old man and the old woman get along fine. Fact is, he's pretty nice to her. Likes to lie with his head on her belly.

Back in 1920 I acted as gun support for Wanda Vik-Persen, the most beautiful big-game camera hunter I ever saw. Copper-haired, gray-eyed, with a smile that made a fellow want to go out and get scalps for her. We took pictures of rhinos at Lake Natron, at the base of Mount Kenya, along the Uaso Nyiro as far as Lorian Swamp. She was strictly an amateur photographer, and the only game pictures I ever knew her to sell were a few shots to

Near-sighted, aggressive, and endangered: mother and child in Tanzania.

Sir Abe Bailey, a Johannesburg mining and racing man.

Mrs. Vik-Persen would stand looking into the viewing plate while the big beasts approached, sometimes at a gallop, until they were within fifteen—yes, ten—yards of her. Then she'd snap the shutter and skip out of the way. She drove me almost crazy. Lots of times if I'd shot when she bulbed the shutter, the beast would have fallen on top of her. But there was never an accident. She'd watch the big brutes trot off with their silly tails straight up and say: "Look at the old darlings!"

For sheer guts, give me camera hunters instead of bloodletters every time. After working with Cameraman Bob Schlick, I've never been the same. Still, we never had serious trouble. I think God must have a fondness for camera hunters.

During my 1937 trip to Africa, while I was shooting rhino specimens on the fringes of marshes around Lake Natron in Tanganyika for a scientist, a bull rhino gave me one of the biggest laughs I ever had. We had made camp not far from a game trail, and occasionally rhinos and elephants would meander past without giving us a glance. The scientist was a Dr. Watrous from Memphis. He was studying the internal organs of animals. He would dig into a carcass, extract the liver, kidneys, and almost everything else he could remove, weigh them, measure them, then put them in big jars containing preservative fluid. When he did his work out in the open, it wasn't so bad, but sometimes he would have livers and lungs all over camp. We finally persuaded him to put up a bell tent not far from the game trail and to work in there.

One afternoon we got the tent up, carried his specimens to it, and helped him stack the jars in neat piles. He went about his work, humming happily. Just before dusk a bull rhino came along, saw the tent, decided to investigate, and walked up close, sniffing and snorting. Doc Watrous went out under the flap on the other side.

The rhino approached until his nose was almost touching the canvas. Nobody wanted to shoot him, and anyway, we figured he'd take himself off after he had satisfied his curiosity. Then the breeze got in under the flap where Watrous had come out. It bellied the tent with a sudden puff and a sort of clapping sound.

Snorting in alarm, the rhino backed away, got on his mark, and attacked the tent like a bulldozer. He took out the center pole in his rush, and the canvas collapsed on him. The camp was suddenly a bedlam. Kaffirs shouted; Doc Watrous jumped up and down, screaming. The tent heaved and bounded and rolled as if filled with explosions. The rhino, strangely enough, made no vocal noises. I guess he was too scared. He seemed to fall on his side. When he got to his feet, he popped right through the canvas. He had liver and kidneys all over him and was sprinkled with glass.

He trotted off, changing his direction every two or three jumps. He was so bewildered he didn't know where he was going.

Doc Watrous was like a man struck witless. He stood there in his white butcher's robe, looking first at the wreck of the tent, then at the disappearing rhino. He picked up a short stick and scratched his chest. Then he picked up a campstool, sat on it, and looked at me.

"Son of a bitch," he said.

This Doc Watrous figured in another funny incident. That is, it was funny to us. Not to him. It was way back in off the Congo River, not too far from Yambuya. We had shot him an elephant. Doc had sawed a big hole in its side and after taking out a couple of hundred pounds of organs had crawled inside the carcass looking for something or other that elephants have inside them.

We had set up a big balance scale a few feet from the dead beast's rear. The scale hung from a tripod about ten feet high. While Doc was crawling about inside the carcass, one of the Kaffirs fell against a leg of the tripod and the whole contraption fell across the elephant just as Doc shoved his head up into the open. He saw it coming and ducked back into the bloody interior. The top of the tripod fell across the hole in the beast's side. When Doc ducked down inside, he must have buried his face in a pool of blood, for now as he stuck his head up between the legs of the tripod his face was a bloody mess. As he sputtered and spat, the two tripod legs closed gently on his neck, pinning him neatly.

Black Rhino with tickbirds.

We rescued him, and as I finished wiping blood from his face he looked at me with a worried expression. "You know," he said, "I believe I'm accident-prone."

Doc Watrous did seem jinxed. I've never been charged by a rhino except when I deliberately pestered one for some camera hunter or for a sportsman who wouldn't shoot a "sitting duck." But Watrous was charged three times on three successive days, each time escaping by some high powered dodging. The last time this happened the rhino had his choice of coming after a Kikuyu gunbearer, me, or Watrous. He chose Doc. As I watched the man and beast race around a mimosa tree, it suddenly came to me why rhinos picked on Watrous. He always wore a white jacket or a white helmet, or both. When he began wearing khaki, the rhinos passed him up.

A man learns—if he lives long enough.

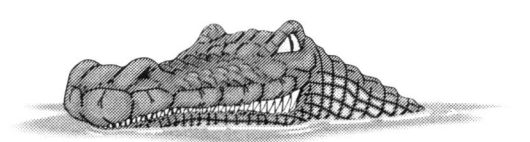

CROCODILES

C ROCODILES are the ugliest, cruelest, most loathsome eaters of men and beasts in Africa. All the time they're watching you hungrily with glassy green eyes they're also smiling slyly at you with reptilian mouths. You know if they get you they'll not eat you while you're nice and fresh but will drag you down to the bottom of the river, tear you to pieces, and shove the pieces in mud, there to remain until you rot. For crocodiles cannot masticate and must wait until their larger kills are putrid before they can swallow them.

Except when wounded or starving they seldom attack openly but sneak up on you under water, their feet drawn tight against their sides, their tails propelling them as swiftly and silently as the shadow of death. They usually grab an arm or a leg, then drag you down to where your shrieks become only agonized, choking gulps.

My first experience with crocs seems funny now, but it wasn't funny at the time. It was in the days before penicillin, when African hunters sometimes treated their wounds by keeping them moist with a weak solution of salt and boiled water while exposing them to sunlight. That's how it happened that one late December afternoon I was lying naked on top of a flat sugar-loaf rock which rose three feet out of the dried mud on a bank of a branch of the Nengo River in the northwest tip of Rhodesia.

The day before, I'd fallen on sharp rocks and gouged some meat out of my right thigh. My khaki pants had been driven into the wound, and I was trying to prevent infection. I was alone. Ubusuku and two Bechuana boys, Bill and Oka, had saddled the riding oxen and gone upriver to look for a couple of ornithologists from the Moscow Rumiantsov Museum who were supposed to have met us at this spot.

The rock on which I lay was about eight feet long and three feet wide. The stream was just a series of pools swarming with hungry crocodiles, for with the drying of the rivers the fish had disappeared, and fish are the crocodile's chief item of diet. All up and down the branches of the Nengo crocs had taken to pulling in calves, bucks—anything that came near the river's brink. In some areas children playing along the banks had been dragged in and devoured by the stinking reptiles.

About fifteen feet behind the rock on which I dozed was a four-foot-high crocodile's egg nest made of mud and decaying vegetable matter. I thought nothing of it, for what I didn't know about crocs would have filled a book.

The day was slightly cool, but the rock was warm. I lay on my left side, my head on my arm, my rifle beside me, and slept. After a while I dreamed I was back in the States listening to the noises of a litter of setter puppies I once owned. I moved, and the clatter of my rifle as I kicked it over the edge of the rock wakened me. I realized abruptly that I wasn't in Michigan, but in the Congo Basin country—stark naked.

Not fully awake, I slid over off the rock to retrieve my rifle and stepped on something soft and wiggly that yelped. I tried to jump, slipped, and sat down hard—not on the ground, but on three or four newly hatched baby crocodiles. About sixty of the little ten-inch devils surrounded me. Their mother, who'd been herding her brood to water after opening the dirt mound to let them out, was up on her toes, not twenty feet away, glaring at me.

Everything happened at once. About six of the nasty little yellow-eyed demons, part of the egg yolk still sticking to their bellies, attacked my toes, heels, and calves with needle-sharp teeth and savage, puppy-like yelps. I grabbed up my rifle and got back on the rock just a second before the mother cut loose with a choking cough and made a swipe at me with her tail. She missed.

She almost turned a back somersault to get at me with her jaws, but I shoved the muzzle of my .303 inside her mouth and squeezed the trigger. She collapsed. I put another shot in her neck where the green of her back shaded to the yellow of her throat. She went limp as a dead snake. By this time all the croc babies I hadn't squashed had disappeared into the nearest pool. I began scraping egg yolk and assorted squashings from my backside, but the "dead" mother flipped her tail, yawned a couple of times, and began crawling toward the river. I shot her again behind the jaws. She kept crawling slowly, draggingly. Then I really drilled her—four shots close to her eye.

I went up the bank and downstream about one hundred yards to our outspan and washed myself clean with drinking water. I slipped on my clothes and went back to look at my croc. She was gone. At first I thought she'd risen from the dead, but spoor showed she'd been dragged into the pool by a couple of old bulls. They'd eat her eventually.

All I knew about crocodiles up to that time were hunters' and Kaffirs' tales. Crocs were just crocs to me. But the day those little fiends nipped me with their immature teeth, my education started. Next morning every one of the thirty-three tiny punctures began to fester. I treated them like snakebites—cut them open with my knife, let them bleed, then gave them the salt-water-and-sunlight treatment. In a week they were healed.

Crocodiles in some rivers are more savage than those in other streams. I've never heard a reasonable explanation for this. Also, in some rivers, crocs do not tear you to pieces before shoving you into the mud to rot. They shove you in whole and do not eat your carcass until it floats. Crocodiles in the Nengo River are vicious, determined killers. The Nengo flows into the Zambezi River, as does the Lungwebungu, but about sixty miles to the south. Crocodiles in the Lungwebungu can be cleared from around a ford by beating the water with long sticks. Try that on some stretches of the

Nengo, and you'll have every croc within a half mile coming to see what's going on. Yet they are the same "straight-nosed" crocs—adults averaging from eleven to fifteen feet in length.

Farther west in the coastal rivers of Angola the crocs are "pug-nosed." That is, their noses turn up. But they're every bit as evil, ugly, and loathsome as their straight-nosed brothers.

Crocodile hunting has always been a reasonably profitable business if you have cheap transportation for the skins. In Uganda crocodile hunting has long been a going industry, but today the British Government is doing everything possible to make it Big Business. With a goal of a thousand crocs a month, the Uganda Fish Marketing Corporation, Ltd. has been opening markets in the United States for skins and developing hide-processing industries in the British Isles. Hunters are needed, but don't start off to shoot crocs until you've written for all the dope to the Uganda Fish Marketing Corporation, Ltd., Kampala, Uganda Protectorate, British East Africa. They'll tell you about licenses required, best gun calibers, and prices paid for raw skins.

At present the Uganda crocodile project is centered chiefly the reed-lined shores of Lake Kyoga, but trading posts are being established throughout the protectorate. My suggestion is that you make your crocodile safari to the streams and shore flats of the Semliki Valley south of Lake Albert. There are really crocs in them there waters! However, all the lakes and rivers of Uganda teem with them.

Uganda belongs to the black man, and the whites

in authority intend to see that it remains that way. It's the only spot on earth where the people native to the country are protected from exploitation by greedy colonists. No white man in Uganda may undertake anything that would violate the rights of the natives. In Uganda there is no pushing around of the blacks such as we Americans gave the Indians; or as the Boers gave, and are giving, the natives of South Africa; or as the whites and the East Indians of Kenya and Tanganyika are giving the Masai and other tribes. If you're the type of white man who can't give the black man an even break, stay away from Uganda.

My trip to the Nengo River country, however, was not for the purpose of shooting crocodiles. I went there to shoot birds for the Rumiantsov Museum. I had signed a contract with the museum's agent in Bulawayo and was told to meet their two scientists, Awyang and Di Giovanni, on the third southern branch of the Nengo. Ubusuku, the Bechuanas, and I made the six-hundred mile trip from Bulawayo by ox wagon and outspanned at the rendezvous. Awyang and Di Giovanni hadn't shown up by the next noon, and figuring they might have missed us, I sent Ubusuku, Bill, and Oka in search of them.

It was five days before they showed up with the missing scientists. The two men had been lost. They had come in from Benguela on the Angola coast with a native guide who had disappeared one night with a sixty-pound load of salt. If Ubusuku hadn't located them, they probably never would have showed up, for if ever there were two babes in the woods, it was these two.

Dr. Hohang Awyang, in charge of the expedition, was an American-educated Chinese ornithologist—a good one. He was smart, patient, and obliging. He'd brought a list of more than three hundred birds his museum wanted. Gennaro di Giovanni was an Italian taxidermist, a conceited, nasty-tongued little firecracker. He was about the dirtiest white man I ever saw; seldom changed his clothes, seldom bathed, but took good care of his long waxed black mustache. He tried to keep it smoothly tapered, but it was always unraveling at the ends, and his fingers were constantly twisting and pulling at it.

I shot birds for the next three months. But when the crocodiles weren't running us ragged, Di Giovanni was. I'd trail a rare bird for hours, get him lined up in my sights, only to have Di Giovanni yell:

"No shoota the head. No shoota the chest. Shoota the guts."

If his yapping didn't frighten the bird away, it would throw me off my shot. If it hadn't been that I knew Awyang was enduring Di Giovanni for the good of the expedition, there were times when I'd have choked the little magpie.

Among the birds Awyang wanted were bee eaters, white-breasted scissorbills, red-beaked scissorbills, white spoonbills, black geese, knobbed-beak geese, green pigeons, red-breasted trogons, long-legged avocets, Numidian cranes, white buffalo birds, and an assorted lot of plovers, ducks, snipes, herons, sand martins, swallows, speckled kingfishers, blue-and-orange kingfishers, ibis, and fish hawks.

It was about the toughest shooting I ever undertook. First of all, just any pair of birds wouldn't do. They had to be male and female, just the right size and just the right coloring. Awyang would pass up hundreds of birds before pointing out one he wanted. Di Giovanni skinned and mounted them right there in the wilderness.

Di Giovanni was an excellent taxidermist. It was a pleasure to watch him bending over a tiny bird, his scalpels, bone saws, forceps, and brain scoops laid out in a glittering row on a white towel. But if one of my shots had broken a back, a breastbone, or nicked a skull, his tirade didn't end until his mustache unwound and hung down like a pair of walrus tusks.

Because the birds had to be killed with as little damage to their skins and feathers as possible, I used more guns than a playboy sportsman after big game. I had a single-shot, bolt-action Remington .22; a 20-gauge shotgun; a 12-bore single-barreled quarter-choke Powell; and my .303.

The .22 was used on small birds like starlings, sand martins, bee eaters, and buffalo birds; the 20-gauge for green pigeons, speckled kingfishers, and birds of that size. The 12-gauge for cranes, fish hawks, bustards, flying geese, ducks, and plovers; the .303 for occasional long shots, particularly at *aasvogelen* (vultures) and knobbed-beak geese.

At least that's what they were supposed to be used for, but more and more I found myself using the .303 and the Powell on crocodiles. They came close to ruining the whole bird project.

They got one of our donkeys, almost killed Di Giovanni, took a hefty bite out of Bill's leg, and finally ganged up and scared us almost witless.

January was supposed to be a wet month in that part of Africa, but it rained only one week. That was enough, however, to overflow the Nengo and its tributaries; the waters poured into flats and meadows, turning them into sloughs and marshes three and four feet deep. Fish left the main streams to feed among the inundated grasses. The crocodiles followed the fish.

As most of the birds hung out in the red bean, pink plum, mother of morning, mimosa, and thorn trees that bordered the river, it was almost impossible to kill one without having it fall in water. The crocs didn't often bother dead birds, but they sure made it tough on anyone who went in to retrieve them.

One morning we were watching the sandbanks along the river for red-beaked scissorbills. They're beautiful birds with snow-white breasts, black backs, and red beaks. They build their nests in hollows in the sand. They're afraid of nothing, attacking crows, hawks, and storks with gusto. But when a man comes along, they droop one wing and pretend to be lame. The upper half of the beak is shorter than the lower. They feed at night on insects which they scoop from the water by skimming along with the protruding underbill just touching the surface.

It was no problem to get scissorbills. The problem was to get two with their beaks the exact shade of red that Awyang wanted. It seems that birds, like dogs, are judged by points, and a certain red hue in a scissorbill's beak was very much desired.

When Awyang spotted exactly the bird he wanted, Di Giovanni, standing beside his donkey, got very excited. He sang his old song:

"No shoota the head. No shoota the chest. Shoota the guts."

I said, "Shut up," and reached for the .22. The little BB-like bullet went through the stomach. The bird should have dropped like a stone. Instead, it lifted its long wings, rose above the sandbank, then volplaned into the marsh, landing with a splash in the center of the slough.

Di Giovanni began shoving Oka toward the water, screaming: "Go get heem. Go get heem."

The Kaffir jumped aside and said sullenly: "Too many crocs."

Di Giovanni flared angrily, picked up a stick, and struck the boy across the face. Then he jumped on his donkey and whipped the animal into the water. He was within feet of the scissorbill when the donkey screamed and went under. Di Giovanni came up spluttering. There was a swirl of white water, the heaving and splashing of dark bodies, then a string of rising bubbles as a croc dragged the donkey off under water.

In the meantime, Ubusuku had raced for the boat about one hundred yards along the slough. Oka and I splashed to Di Giovanni's rescue. I held my .303 high and pushed as fast as I could through the thigh-deep water. Oka, however, moved ahead of me and reached Di Giovanni while I was still about thirty yards away. Instead of attempting to help the screeching Italian, Oka grabbed him around the neck and shoved him under. I yelled, threw my rifle to my shoulder, intending to shoot the Kaffir unless he let loose; but before I could get the sights on him he abruptly disappeared beneath the surface, where he and Di Giovanni put on a struggle something like that of the croc and the donkey.

I don't remember what happened the next minute or so. All I know is that I dropped my rifle, reached down and got hold of the Italian, and jerked him above water. He was blue-lipped and limp. Oka got to his feet, grinning. I threw Di Giovanni belly down across my shoulder and started jiggling him violently. Water spurted from his mouth every time his stomach bumped my heaving shoulder. He moaned faintly, then began to struggle. Next Ubusuku and Awyang were beside us in our folding boat.

I dumped Di Giovanni face down in the boat and grabbed for Oka. Awyang said quietly: "Let him alone."

I looked at the Chinese. He said: "If the Italian had struck me across the face, I'd have killed him myself."

"Oka attacked a white man. He has to be punished."

Awyang looked at me without smiling. "The boy was in the right," he said.

I picked up the dead scissorbill and kicked around in the mud until I located my rifle. We helped Di Giovanni back to camp and laid him on his blankets. He began to cry. Awyang and I walked away and left him weeping.

My sympathies were also with Oka, but white man's prestige must be maintained, so I fired him. Then I paid him an extra two pounds to send me a boy to take his place. He sent a Hottentot boy called Bumpo.

The good weather held and we got lots of bird specimens. The river kept lowering, and its pools grew smaller. The hippos, who normally live at peace with crocs, refused to let them share the pools any longer, so the crocs moved permanently into the shallow sloughs. Hippos grazed in the dank grasses along these marshes, and their gruntings and bellowings, mixed with the champings and coughings of the crocs, filled every hour of the night.

Bumpo was always shaking his head and warning us that "something bad is going to happen," but when we tried to get him to tell us what he feared, he'd only roll his eyes.

Ubusuku, usually cheerful and willing, now became morose. His pride was hurt because he was working for a hunter who had taken a sissy job shooting birds. And he didn't like crocodile shooting any better. He classed crocs with snakes, and to a Zulu, nothing is lower than a snake. One morning, unable to bear it any longer, he said:

"*Baas*, men who stay in the kraal to milk cows soon grow breasts like women."

"Cheer up, Ubusuku," I answered. "This job will last only until after the heavy rains. Then we'll be off after elephants."

With brooding eyes searching the flat margins of the slough, he said: "The lion who lives on grass grows ears like a rabbit."

He spotted a big croc dozing in the sun. "Look, *Baas*," he said, "I will show you that hunting crocodiles with a gun is work fit only for fat women."

He grabbed a short stabbing assagai and a long spear, which he kept leaning against a tree when in camp, and bounded into the waist-high grass. About fifty yards from the croc, he flopped on his belly. I didn't see a sign of him—not even a quivering of the grass—until he suddenly appeared beside the croc and drove his spear into the side of its throat. The croc, spear dangling, stood on its tail, opened its jaws, roared, and flopped over on its back. Ubusuku was instantly beside it, thrusting, stabbing, thrusting with the short assagai in one hand while he pulled his long spear out of the croc with the other.

The brute whirled about and rushed for the water. Ubusuku hurled the spear. It sank deep in the croc's side. Bellowing like a bull, the croc went up on its tail again, spun, and fell into the water. It dived, came up a few yards away, and with flailing tail began a mad, erratic rushing about. Ubusuku, his assagai held high, jumped in after it. Rifle in hand, I headed for the battle at a run. When I reached the water's edge, Ubusuku was about twenty-five yards out, his assagai poised. The croc went under and almost instantly broke water, coughing, the rows of long fangs gleaming wetly in its half-open mouth. It foamed straight for Ubusuku. I threw up the rifle.

"*Ikona!* No! No!" Ubusuku yelled, and dived under the charging reptile. He came up behind it and a little to one side. Evading the wildly slapping tail, he lurched forward, grabbed a foreleg, and began stabbing, stabbing, stabbing.

A wild flurry threw Ubusuku clear, and the croc dived. Ubusuku crawled ashore at my feet, panting. The croc came up about fifty yards out, turned over on its back, and jerkily stiffened its legs. For a few moments it held them straight up. Then they folded slowly against its sides and, still on its back, the croc sank out of sight.

"So that's woman's work," I said. "Now, you big heathen, tell me why you *really* don't like to hunt crocs."

"They stink."

And stink they do, but just the same, they're good eating. Ubusuku wouldn't touch their flesh, of course, but the rest of us enjoyed an occasional crocodile snack. Young crocs taste best.

Crocodile stink is a particularly offensive form of musk. It's produced in four glands, two in the sides of the throat and two in the rectum. When the reptile is calm, the glands are closed slits, but when he is excited, angry, frightened, or hot for a lady croc, the glands turn inside out, puff up like pink ping-pong balls, and exude their foul essence.

The odor clings to whatever it touches, with astonishing tenacity. As the crocs crawl along the bottoms of rivers, the musk leaves a trail which other crocs follow. When in the throes of sexual desire, male crocs bellow at intervals all night long and, with each bellow, taint the air with squirts of mephitic perfume. When they've made enough noise and created enough stench, the female crocs capitulate with blissful grins on their evil faces.

In periods between hunting trips I did game studies and nature articles for European newspapers such as the London *Daily Mail,* Berlin *Deutsche Allgemeine Zeitung,* and Budapest *Pester Lloyd.* I wanted to do a couple of pieces about crocodiles and asked Di Giovanni to dissect one for me. He refused.

To prevent corrosion, the Italian kept his beloved taxidermy instruments embedded in a forty-pound can of lard. Now and then the lard would get rancid and Di Giovanni would cook it to sweeten it. One evening as the lard was bubbling, the pot tipped and lard poured into the flames. It blazed like petrol. Di Giovanni took it hard. I felt sorry for him. There was no fresh lard nearer than Bulawayo, five hundred miles away.

Next morning I went out, got a hippo, and had the Kaffirs boil about fifty pounds of its fat in water. For about twenty hours it simmered and was skimmed often. When cooled, it was as nice and firm a "lard" as Di Giovanni had ever seen. He was so happy to get it that he promised to dissect my croc for me.

I shot a big bull within the hour. The first thing Di Giovanni did was to take out the heart. He held it in his hands, and I could see it was still palpitating.

"Heart jumpa, huh? You wait," he said.

He wrapped the heart in a damp towel and

placed it in the sun. A half hour later he unwrapped it. It was still palpitating.

With knives, saws, hooks, pinchers, and assorted gadgets he took that croc apart limb by limb and organ by organ. He first made a cut at the base of the skull and lifted off the top of the head. He showed me how the upper jaw was hinged so that it could move and how the unmovable bottom jaw was attached solidly to the skeleton. He showed me the powerful muscles that give the jaws tremendous crushing ability and the comparatively feeble muscles that open the jaws; muscles so weak that a man can hold a croc's mouth closed with his hands—as Ubusuku demonstrated several times.

A croc's tongue is wide and thick, the entire length of its underside fastened to the lower jaw. Near its base it thickens into a large lump which acts as a valve to keep water from going down the throat. The teeth are fangs, running in a double row around the mouth—large teeth in front, smaller ones behind them. The teeth grow continuously, old ones being pushed out by new ones as they come in. One time when prospecting in Uganda for hippo teeth to be made into "human" teeth for dental plates, we found in a dry river pool more than four hundred discarded croc teeth. Ubusuku made them into necklaces by stringing them on wire.

Because of the croc's tied tongue and the spaces between his fangs, he cannot chew. He can, however, swallow an animal the size of a small dog at a gulp. He swallows waterfowl, feathers and all.

Bones mean nothing to him, for he can crush even the largest. Sometimes he eats the bigger game by shredding it. He holds the kill in his teeth and shakes his head from side to side. Guts squirt in all directions; legs, heads, and chunks fly off. He immediately eats the bite-sized pieces but takes larger portions down to his mud larder to rot.

Occasionally two crocs will co-operate in tearing an animal to pieces. Each takes one end. A few tugs and shakes and the carcass really comes apart.

Crocodiles cannot eat under water. When inclined to a snack of something they've stored on the river bottom, they bring up a mouthful, stick their heads above surface, and gulp. It's a nasty sound. So is the noise they make when they snap their empty mouths closed—sounds like someone hitting a drum.

Out of this reptile's stomach Di Giovanni took four large pieces of antelope leg bone, a double handful of pebbles, several stones larger than ducks' eggs, the skull of a bird, and three antelope hoofs. The contents of a croc's belly are not always so ordinary. Once when I opened a female crocodile in the Congo I found a Maria Theresa dollar. So far as I know, the Maria Theresa dollar is used only in Ethiopia, two thousand miles from where I killed that croc. A friend of mine once found an amber pipestem in a croc's stomach. It makes one wonder.

Croc's ears are holes in the head two inches behind the eyes. They're fitted with horny flaps that can be raised and lowered. When a croc is angry or excited, these flaps flutter up and down like hummingbirds' wings. They're closed when he's under water.

The ears are your target for the brain shot—the only shot guaranteed to kill him instantly. A shot through the side of the neck lays him low, but unless it severs the spinal cord it will require more than one bullet to do him in. A bullet through the heart gives him plenty of time to dive to the bottom and get himself lost. Don't shoot him below the line where the dark of his back meets the yellow of his belly. The hide on his sides and stomach is what you sell to leather buyers. No use punching bullet holes in your income.

If you'll give natives the scaly top hide and the meat, they'll skin the reptiles for you without charge. If you give the men of some tribes the croc's heart, they'll not only love you like a brother but will present you with a couple of bunch-bottomed women as a gift. They think that eating the heart gives them courage.

If you're after skins, it's a waste of time to shoot crocs in the water. If you wound them, they dive. If you kill them, they sink. The bigger ones spend most of the warm days basking in sunlight along banks of the rivers. If there's plenty of food in the streams, they'll not stop to argue with you but will head for water at a surprisingly fast run. However, if food is scarce and they've been hungry for some time, they'll attack anything edible. That includes buffalo, lion, rhino, and man. A hungry crocodile often goes a-hunting. I've seen them grab a buffalo calf by the nose one hundred yards from water and drag the struggling brute to doom.

Lions fear nothing in Africa but man and crocodiles. A lion with most of his head inside an fourteen-foot croc's jaws isn't able to do effective fighting.

However, the croc's favorite method of getting prey is to lie hidden among water plants or reeds, sometimes with his nose actually touching the shore. When an animal puts his head down to drink—crunch!

Crocodiles eat more humans than do any other African beasts. Each year they devour hundreds of native children. Black youngsters like to play in water as well as white ones do, and warnings of danger lurking have little effect. Many native women are grabbed while washing clothes at a river's edge or while dipping water from a stream. Men are caught by the arm while paddling a boat; caught by a leg while wading a ford; caught by the head while sipping water at a river's brink; and caught while walking carelessly along sandy or marshy banks.

One can understand natives becoming the prey of crocodiles, for among natives caution is chiefly noticeable by its absence. They don't often think beyond the moment. It's more difficult to understand white men becoming the victims of crocs. That is, until you realize that the average white man in the wilds of Africa is careless, thoughtless, and foolhardy beyond belief.

It's the white man who starves to death, although surrounded by edible barks, grubs, snails, ants, leaves, mice, and roots. It's the white man who goes to bed with his door open in country infested by starving lions; who in crocodile-infested rivers paddles his boat sitting down, hands close to water, instead of standing.

It's the white man who has absolute faith in the killing power of an "artillery-caliber" rifle; who believes the shocking-power of a bullet is the answer to deadly shooting. It's the white man who uses soft-nosed slugs when he should use solid ones, or uses solid ones when he should use soft-noses. It's the white man who dashes into brush after a wounded beast instead of waiting for the wounds to take effect. It's the white man . . .

Take me, for instance. I fell asleep on the low rock within a few feet of a crocodile's nest. I've been lost for hours within a mile of the wagons. Once when being chased by natives who were after my scalp, I rubbed honey on my head and face and squatted in a river, with butterflies swarming so thickly about the honey that my pursuers never found me. What was so dumb about that? Well, as I waded ashore, three crocodiles who'd been dozing on the bank rushed into the water.

The business of getting your hands close to water while in a boat can be bad. One day Bill, the Bechuana boy, was fishing with a hand line from our folding boat. He wasn't far out from the shore of the slough. I was sitting on a hummock watching him as he leaned over the boatside, slowly raising and lowering his baited hook. The air was clear. The surface of the slough was smooth as glass. He pulled a flapping mullet into the boat, rebaited his hook, and dropped it overside again. Beyond him, my eye was held by an approaching low V-shaped swell—a swell such as might be made by the prow of a tiny, fast-moving boat. I watched idly at first as it sped toward Bill, but was on my feet quickly enough when below the apex of the swell I suddenly saw a long, black, rocketing shadow. I fired, but the angle was too great. The bullet slapped the water and whined harmlessly away.

Bill jerked up his arm just as huge, fanged jaws clashed shut in the space where his hand had been a split second before. He stood erect, his paddle raised as if to strike. The croc made a lightning about-turn and with his flattened tail knocked Bill out of the boat. Bill heaved and splashed and stumbled toward shore. His hands were actually on land when the croc grabbed his leg. Bill screamed and was instantly jerked backward into the water.

A moment later he scrambled ashore on his hands and knees. The croc's front teeth had met in the calf of his leg and had jerked through the flesh. I fired four quick shots into the air—our signal for quick help—then applied makeshift tourniquets. Ubusuku and Di Giovanni came running. The Italian did some fast surgery, and Bill got well, but his limp was permanent.

A crocodile's love life is curious. The mating is smelly, noisy, and often follows the murder of another male croc by the husband. For males put on terrific battles at mating time. Two rush together, interlock their jaws, and stage a frightful, plunging, splashing struggle until one of them dies. As soon as the marriage is consummated, the female whirls away with a disdainful flip of her tail. If her mate knows what's good for him, he'll stay away from her, for the love that made her so quiescent turns quickly to hate, and she'll kill him if she can. She seems to realize belatedly that he wanted her to have children only so he could eat them. There's nothing a papa croc enjoys more in the way of food than his kids. He'll even open the nest and eat the eggs if his wife doesn't keep her eye on him.

When thirty to ninety eggs fill her belly, the female croc builds an incubator for them. In areas where nights are warm she digs a two-foot hole in sand, deposits her eggs, and fills in the hole. Warm suns and hot breezes maintain the nest at correct temperatures.

Where nights are cool she lays the eggs on a four-inch-deep layer of mixed dirt and rotting vegetation. She covers the first layer of eggs with the mixture and deposits the rest of the eggs on top. Then she piles more dirt and decomposing leaves and grasses over the whole clutch—and keeps piling it up until she has a mound three to four feet high.

When shooting lab specimens for Dr. Watrous, he told me that crocodile incubators maintain an internal temperature of about 105 degrees day and night, in all kinds of weather. Some native tribes hatch hens' eggs in similar mounds, substituting manure for the vegetation.

Crocodile eggs are eaten with gusto by natives and by many whites. Only the yolk is used. The white of the egg contains no albumin and will not coagulate when cooked. Crocodile eggs are a favorite food of the big monitor lizards. They open the nest and carry off the eggs one at a time, hiding them under a bush until they've stolen them all. Then they stuff themselves until they can barely wiggle. If it weren't for the terrific egg toll taken by men and lizards crocodiles would have overrun Africa long ago.

When time for hatching approaches, the female visits the nest and cocks her ears for sounds of yapping and hiccuping within. When she hears them, she removes the dirt—and there they are, a batch of nasty, snapping, yipping, sharp-toothed, yellow-eyed heads sticking out of shells.

The little devils are hatched with murder in their hearts. With only their jaws out of the egg, they'll bite a finger held too close. Their puppy-like yelps attract male crocs, and the old boys float offshore with drooling mouths. However, the female herds the hatch safely to the water's edge, and from that moment on the youngsters hang out in shallows along river margins where old males can't get at them.

The shell is lined with membrane too tough to break by pushing, so little crocs grow an egg tooth on the top of their noses. With this they cut the membrane and break the outer shell. Shortly after the youngsters hit water the egg tooth drops off.

The eggs are only three inches long, but ten-inch babies emerge. Their bodies are marked with transverse half-inch bands of brown and green. Their yellow eyes are slitted. Part of the egg yolk remains attached to their bellies for a few days; probably an emergency food supply which is seldom needed, for within minutes of hitting the water, youngsters are catching fish by the tails.

Warmth is essential to croc life. In warm waters crocs grow twelve inches a year. Even the largest, should he get into water having a temperature of less than forty-six degrees, loses all muscular activity and drowns. Most adult crocs are rogues and live alone. Young crocs are social and congregate in shallow riverside pools, moving into the main stream only long enough to grab themselves a meal.

When rivers fall because of lack of rain, fish become scarce and hunger stalks among the crocodiles; the big boys get so ravenous that they actually leap at low-flying waterfowl. They surface, lift their tails, and bring them down on the water with a violent slap, at the same time forcing their foreparts upward in a sort of rocking jump. I've seen them grab ducks five to six feet in the air. Wild fowl soon refuse to settle on water when crocs are starving, so the adult crocs invade the shallows and eat all smaller crocs they can catch. They can go a long time without food, but they must eat sooner or later. It's when they come to extremities that they drag themselves out into the flatlands, lie as logs until an animal—any animal—comes close. They grab it by the nose, jerk and pull and tug it to the river, and hold it under until it drowns. The big Nile crocodiles are so powerful that they've been known to capture a fifteen-hundred-pound rhino in this way. The only animal a croc will not attack is the hippo. If he pesters a hippo too much, the hippo simply bites him in two.

Rains continued to hold off until the end of February. Water in sloughs was less than a foot deep, and river pools had become opaque and stagnant. The desperately hungry crocs prowled farther and farther into the flatlands in search of food, but they had little luck, for lions, rhinos, buffalo, and antelope, hitherto plentiful, had disappeared. That should have been the tip-off to me that trouble was brewing, but all it did was make me slightly curious.

The "trouble" came at last. It broke up our bird-hunting expedition and cost us our oxen. I've gone through similar experiences since, but none brought me to the verge of panic as that first one did. I still dream about it occasionally and awake in a sweat.

The trouble hit our outspan just after midnight, March 2. It came in the form of crocs—hundreds of them. That the fear which accompanied their invasion was due to my own ignorance doesn't make the experience less frightening. Here's the way it hit:

We had got all the bird specimens the area afforded and were about to move to the Okavango Swamp country for some rare waterfowl Awyang wanted. Di Giovanni's cases of specimens so filled the wagon that there was no room for our chuck boxes, tents, and other gear. We needed another wagon and ten or twelve more oxen, so Awyang and Bumpo rode two of our oxen sixty miles to Liborta to buy an additional transport outfit.

Di Giovanni was very sick with a bad spell of fever. Bill limped around on a makeshift crutch. Ubusuku and I put in a couple of days cleaning and sorting gear, greasing wagon wheels, sorting and stacking boxes and cans for easy loading.

That night the crocs came. Ubusuku and Bill were asleep beside the dying coals of their fire, their heads wrapped in blankets. I had been asleep, too, but had wakened with a strange feeling of apprehension. It took me a little time to figure out that I missed the roaring of lions, occasional cries of their victims, the booming of disturbed ostriches, barking of zebras—all the noises of an African night on the veldt. Even the chirps, squeaks, and rustling of insects and mice seemed to have stopped. It just wasn't natural.

I went to Di Giovanni's tent, saw he was all right, and went back to my fire. The oxen, trained to sleep behind the wagon, were on their feet, shifting about nervously, their long horns clashing against each other. Abruptly they began backing toward the wagon, their heads all turned toward the river. I threw wood on the fire, picked up the Powell 12-bore, and put a handful of shells loaded with No. 2 buckshot in my pants pocket.

Then I smelled musk—crocodile musk. It reeked. I could taste it. It seemed to drip off my soft palate down my throat and into my stomach. I almost gagged. The oxen got the smell and began bawling. Suddenly they lifted their tails, wheeled in their tracks, and stampeded into the darkness.

Instantly Ubusuku and Bill were on their feet. They sniffed once and grabbed their spears. Came a strange rustling and scraping—a sort of metallic slithering. The new wood on the fire blazed up, and I stared tensely into the blackness. It seemed to me there was movement out there—movement too definite, too sustained to have been caused by flickering flames.

Ubusuku, knobkerrie in one hand, throwing spear in the other, moved toward the curtain of darkness. But he jumped back, booming Zulu curses, as a big crocodile, eyes coldly green, dragged himself slowly into the circle of firelight. I blew in the side of his head with the 12-bore. As I fired, Bill threw a great armful of wood on the fire. Sparks flew and flames leaped high, driving back the night and uncovering a mass of grinning crocs' eyes glowing red and green and orange. I got only a glimpse before the flames lowered, but it seemed to me that the invaders stretched away right and left to infinity.

I realized by this time that here was one of the great crocodile migrations I'd heard of. I knew from hearsay that, once the instinct to migrate took over, nothing but fire would stop their forward movement.

My first impulse was to run. But Di Giovanni was down. Bill's leg wouldn't carry him one hundred yards. My next thought was to hoist Di Giovanni to the top of the wagon-load and for the rest of us to crawl up beside him. But the specimen boxes were fragile. Our weight would crush them and destroy work which might take a year to replace. There was no tree close enough to offer refuge, and anyway, we couldn't have gotten Di Giovanni into a tree.

We had a five-gallon can of petrol left among the stores and three or four five-gallon cans of kerosene. I yelled to Ubusuku to bring them to me.

They were hard to get at among the boxes, and it took him a little while.

The crocs came on, dragging their bellies and tails. I handed Bill the .303. We blazed away, killing eight or nine and wounding some. Crocs behind crawled over those that were hit, slithering off the struggling wounded, but not stopping nor slowing.

Three big ones got to their toes, made a quick, short rush toward us, then flattened themselves on the ground, opened their mouths wide, and froze in that position.

I reached into my pocket for more shells. There were none. I grabbed the .303 from Bill and put one shot into each of two gaping mouths. I turned the rifle on the third croc. The magazine was empty. Both crocs I had just shot reared, fell backward, jerking their legs as if swimming. Slowly the reptiles behind them crawled forward and over the dying ones.

Our shooting had slowed the advance. I figured they had been dragging along at about two miles an hour. Now they almost stopped, but not quite. I got the impression they were bewildered. Individuals turned their heads from side to side, stretched out a little, then drew back.

I didn't know it then, but they had been following the heavy ground scent of their leaders, and the leaders had been stopped by bullets. Again the fire died down and the motionless croc with the wide-open jaws closed his mouth with a hollow "ploomp." His two lower front teeth went through his nose and stuck at least an inch above the tip.

Many crocs' teeth do this. The teeth grow too long and perforate the end of the nose, sticking through when the mouth is closed.

The croc opened his mouth slightly, as if grinning, and began edging forward again. Behind me, Ubusuku yelled, and I turned to see Di Giovanni staggering about in his nightshirt. Ubusuku leaped for him. Di Giovanni ducked and fell close to the fire. I stooped to pick him up, saw he was unconscious, and let him lie.

I thought, "To hell with the specimens," and yelled to Ubusuku and Bill to lift Di Giovanni to the top of the wagonload. It was too late. Crocs in the van had already reached the wagon and were pushing doggedly forward.

All this while I had been in a sort of half panic. Now I noticed that the crocs had split into two files, skirting the fire on both sides and joining into a single front again when clear of the heat. This left us a circular oasis about eighty feet in diameter with the fire at its center.

Ubusuku and Bill, however, were beyond one of the files of crocs. Ubusuku could have leaped across the plodding reptiles by himself, but he picked Bill up and, holding him in his arms like a baby, used crocs' backs for stepping stones. In three hops he set Bill down safely in the firelit circle. The stepped-on crocs didn't even grunt.

Now that I had time to think, I felt like a fool. My idea had been to pour petrol on the crocs and set it afire, but now I realized that such an idea was that of a frightened idiot. First of all, there was no telling what the burning crocs would do. If they stampeded, they were just as apt to hurl their blazing bodies at the wagon, tents, and gear as anywhere else. Furthermore, the veldt was dry as tinder and a grass fire could have cooked all of us.

I stood there watching crocs move past, thinking, as old Nicobar Jones used to say: "There ain't no bad luck. There's only ignorance."

Oh well, I was young in those days.

I threw wood on the fire. As it blazed up, several crocs got up on their toes, made that funny little forward rush, sank to the ground, and remained absolutely motionless, jaws wide, teeth gleaming. As the fire died, they joined the procession again.

I guess four or five hundred crocodiles wormed past us. They neither feared nor threatened us. They just bellied on their way, dragging their tails behind them. I know now that we could have sat down among them and they'd have ignored us. They had but one thing on their minds, and that was to get to the main stream of the Nengo before dawn.

When the last of them passed, I said to Ubusuku: "All those crocs are at least half-grown. Wonder where the youngsters are?"

"There is plenty of food in the low pools for the small crocs."

I said: "If we'd left them alone, there'd have been no trouble."

"When a hyena breaks wind, O *Baas,* he runs, thinking lions are chasing him."

I didn't answer him.

When Awyang and Bumpo returned with the new wagon and oxen, we split the beasts into two spans of eight oxen each and took off for Bulawayo.

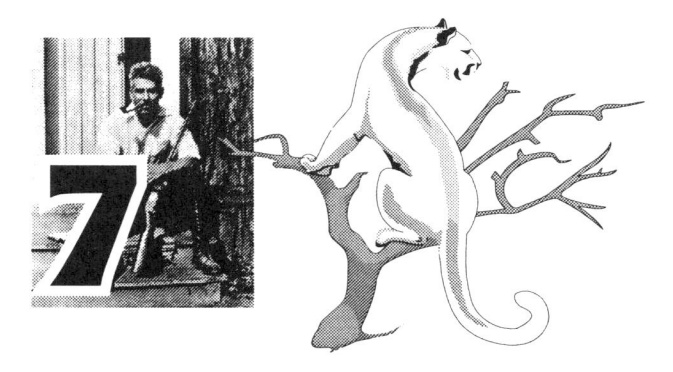

MORE LIONS

I KNOW exactly what happened to twenty-three men in tragic encounters with African lions. Eight of those men were horribly mauled. Six of them lie buried in the cemetery at Nairobi. Graves of nine others are far scattered among the purple-and-silver silences of Africa

Each man was mauled or killed through his own fault because he was ignorant, or careless, or reckless, or a poor shot, or hysterical, or dependent on native gunbearers for support. These are the six deadly shortcomings of lion hunting. Perhaps the best way to explain them is to take some of those twenty-three tragedies apart.

George Grey was the scion of a noble English family. He possessed all six of the deadly shortcomings. He was out after lions with Sir Alfred Pease, one of Africa's most publicized hunters. Six other men were also in the party. All were mounted. Now a horse is slow freight compared to a lion. Pease had warned all members of the party not to approach a lion closer than two hundred yards. But

Grey was overeager. He rode after a shaggy male who was ambling off about his own business.

The lion paid no attention to the pounding hoofs behind him until Grey was within ninety yards, when without warning, the lion whirled and charged. Ninety yards! A lion can do a hundred yards from a standing start in *four seconds* flat. I know. I've timed them. Martin Johnson, who has photographed more lions than any other wild-animal photographer, says that the lion can do a hundred yards from a running start in *three seconds.*

Grey's lion was coming at him at a speed of twenty-five yards every second. He was doing it in forty-five-foot jumps. Ninety yards—270 feet—six jumps! Grey leaped from his horse and let off his first shot at twenty-five yards. He let off his second shot at five yards. Figure it out. Less than four-fifths of a second between shots. That means he was using a heavy-caliber double rifle. It also means that the second shot was a flash shot, for no human can recover from the recoil of one of those big rifles and let off a second *aimed* shot that fast.

Both shots hit, but the lion never faltered. One fifth of a second after Grey's last shot, the lion was tearing at him with claws and teeth. One minute later three of Grey's companions galloped up and each slapped a bullet into the lion from ten yards. They were close enough to have made successful brain shots, but because they were believers in the "shock treatment," they slammed their slugs into the beast's guts. Instead of slowing him, those shots increased his fury and he began mauling

Grey unmercifully. Pease arrived in a rush, dismounted, placed the muzzle of his rifle against the side of the lion's head, and killed him.

The tragedy began as a simple situation. The lion had been ambling away. Any man who could shoot at all could have crippled, perhaps killed, the animal with a backside shot. The backside shot is one of the best. It often punctures the guts, liver, kidneys, lungs, and sometimes gets the heart. If it's a bit off and gets a back leg, it ties the lion down. It's true that lions can get along on three legs for a while, but their flashing speed is gone. Hit in a back leg, a lion may turn at bay or he may head for brush; but he won't attempt a charge until the hunter gets within leaping distance.

If he turns toward the hunter, he's wide open for a chest shot. Aim an inch or two below the base of his throat. His heart is low in his chest. Of course you could make a head shot, but you'll probably want the head for a trophy, and it's a shame to damage it. Anyway, the head shot is a dangerous one for uncertain marksmen. Men have died because they thought there was some skull in that great mop of hair. There isn't. The lion has hardly any skull above the eyes.

Grey and his companions couldn't have made more mistakes if they'd held a conference for the purpose. And Grey might be alive today if his companions hadn't slapped those three useless shots into the lion. Up to that moment the lion was chewing on Grey's arm and shoulder. The chances are that he was about through with mauling, for a lion's anger ebbs quickly once his victim is down.

Even when two of the beasts put on one of their earth-shaking battles over a female, the victor's rage vanishes instantly once his opponent is whipped.

However, those three gut shots made Grey's death certain. I wonder how many men must die before sportsmen learn that *you can't kill a lion with shock.* And I wonder how many men must die before hunters learn the anatomies of the animals they're hunting; learn the location of the heart and brain, at least.

Not long ago I was sitting around a campfire with five deer hunters in California. They were talking about heart shots. I listened awhile, then asked: "Just where is a deer's heart?" All five told me, and all five were wrong. They all had the heart too high. A deer's heart is in the lower third of the chest, a good handbreadth back of the foreleg. Hearts of most other animals are in the same area.

Grey couldn't shoot accurately. He let off his first shot when the charging beast was twenty-five yards away. That means that it was in the middle of the lion's next to the last jump. Any man who can't put a bullet into a lion's chest at twenty-five yards when the animal's coming head on shouldn't be hunting big game. Grey's first slug went through the fleshy part of the lion's shoulder, expanded and tore a nasty furrow along the animal's side. The second shot, at five yards, got the beast as it reared high in its final leap. It entered the stomach just behind the breastbone.

Now if Grey had fired his first shot at ninety yards and his second at sixty yards and they had done the same damage Grey still would have had made another mistake. He had gone with a double rifle and no second gun handy, emergency. Unless you're a whiz with a rifle, you need a minimum of five bullets in your gun if you're going to shoot at a lion. Only a few old professionals consistently drop a lion with a first shot. The average sportsman takes four shots before he gets one in that lays a lion low. And if he's wise, he has a support gunner beside him just in case.

Personally, I like a ten-cartridge magazine. That's one of the reasons I prefer a military Lee-Enfield .303. Ten cartridges in the magazine and one in the chamber. Eleven shots. And there have been times when I needed them all.

It's true that the double rifle is the fastest-shooting gun made—for two shots. But by the time you grab your second gun (if the gunbearer is still there) and let off two more shots, your four-shot total is slower than four shots with a bolt-action rifle.

How fast can a man shoot a bolt- or lever-action gun and still do an accurate job? Well, I held some snap-and-rapid African championships. My best work was eleven bulls' eyes at two hundred yards in thirty-six seconds. I used a Lee-Enfield .303 and worked the bolt without taking the butt from my shoulder. I used a wide V back sight.

There's no place in dangerous game shooting for telescope, small-peep, narrow, or buckhorn sights. I never could see why a man wanted a telescope sight unless his eyes were poor. Anyway, these sights catch in grass, twigs, vines, and everything else that scrapes along the barrel. On small game in open plain, there's no objection to them. The large peep sight is all right. A small peep blurs.

I've known the best lion men in Africa. Almost without exception they use a wide V back sight. Aiming with a wide V is as natural as pointing your finger. You merely see that the tip of the fore sight lines up level with the back-sight shoulders so that it makes a perfect 'W' out of the V. Tilting the barrel is bad business, and a man simply can't tilt the barrel unknowingly with a wide V back sight.

Trigger squeeze is everything. The pull should be adjusted to the man. I like a three-pound pull for game. Some professionals like five pounds. That's too much for a light rifle. A hair trigger doesn't help a man's shooting and may kill someone.

It's possible that Grey waited until the last couple of jumps because he thought the lion was bluffing. Four times out of five a lion's charge is a bluff. He's not really angry, but trying to frighten you away. There's a difference in a lion's charges. When he means business, he comes full-tilt. He uses all of his terrific speed. When he's trying only to scare you, he comes more leisurely—at about one hundred yards in ten seconds.

Let's suppose you think a lion is bluffing and that you do not want to kill him. Your best bet is to stand motionless until he's about twenty-five yards from you. If he's bluffing, he'll stop about there and switch his tail at you. If he doesn't stop, let him have it. If you think he's bluffing and you don't feel like waiting to find out, and if there's a bush handy, step behind it. Once you're out of his sight, he'll probably be satisfied and forget you.

In any case, *do not talk*. There's something about the human voice that stirs rage in the hearts of some lions. You may be standing watching a peaceful family group lying under a tree. They see you, but except for an occasional lifting of their lips they ignore you. You speak, and instantly one gets to his feet, stiffens his tail, and rushes you. One of the problems of professional guides is how to keep clients from speaking at wrong times.

Occasionally a lion that has stopped his rush and is staring at the hunter will be goaded into a genuine charge because someone starts talking. As for yelling at the brutes—well, I'll tell you about Orlando.

Orlando was an American Portuguese. I took him into Bechuanaland to the Okavango Swamp country for some big-game shooting. Incidentally, if you want to save money, do your hunting in Bechuanaland. You can bag the entire list of game, except elephants, at a total cost of about six hundred dollars—licenses and all—and there's no limit on lions and leopards.

Orlando was a short, dark, hard-talking hombre. His jaw stuck out like a crag. He liked to talk about fist fights he'd had and always ended his yarns by saying: "So I bopped him." On a rhino and a buffalo he did all right, but at his first sight of a lion he hurled his rifle at it. The beast was at least 150 yards away.

I said: "What's the matter? Snake bite you?"

He stared at me for a moment, turned to look at the lion, saw it moving slowly in our direction, then grabbed me by the arms from behind and started pushing. I jerked loose. He began yelling.

The lion, which I don't believe had seen us up to that time, stopped, flipped his tail straight up three or four times, and came a-barreling. As I lifted my rifle, Orlando grabbed me again and began shaking me. So *I* bopped *him*.

The lion came within about fifty yards, then changed direction and galloped toward some brush. I let him go. Orlando got to his feet, a bit groggy but sane.

"Once when I was a kid," he said, "our cat scratched me and I got hysterical like this. Ever since, even a kitten gives me the willies."

"Well," I told him, "you can cure it. Just face up to the next lion. Better yet, let's go and get this one."

He shook his head. "Just get me back to Bulawayo."

So back to Bulawayo we went.

I've seen several men who had an unreasonable fear of one beast or another. Some of them acted every bit as hysterical as Orlando did. Most of them cured themselves by standing up to their particular *bête noire* the next time they had a chance. That takes guts.

Never run from a charging lion. If two men are facing a lion and one man runs, the lion will take after him, passing up the man who stands quietly. Four of the twenty-three died while running from charging lions. One of the four, an Irishman named

Wisdom, had just seen his lion run down a bull giraffe. He knew that a giraffe does a hundred yards in five seconds. He knew that the lion had caught up with the bull in six or seven jumps. Yet when pressure was on, Wisdom ran. He didn't have a chance, of course. His partner, who'd stood his ground, got the lion, but not before the brute had broken Wisdom's neck with a sweep of his paw.

But let's get back to Grey. It's obvious that his troubles stemmed from the fact that he couldn't shoot straight. He wasn't in a panic. If he'd been in a panic, he wouldn't have waited until the lion was two jumps from him. He must have known he was no dead shot, otherwise why the big-caliber rifle? No, he made the sad error of thinking that shock would kill a lion. I repeat: *It won't.* Neither will it kill a buffalo.

Grey's fatal encounter took place on open plain. The grass was short, so he could have shot at almost any distance. If the grass had been high, the lion would have stalked him to within fifteen or twenty yards before charging. That, of course, would have been an entirely different setup. Only a man with a suicide urge or one who is just plain nuts will hunt lion in shoulder-high grass. Two of the twenty-three made that mistake.

Those two were Englishmen of a type one often reads about but seldom sees. Their names were St. Leger and Meagher, pronounced "Silinger" and "Mar." They were fine old fellows who wore wrapped cloth puttees, green riding pants, and pleated shooting jackets; they smoked big curved-stem pipes and drank great quaffs of whiskey which they called "nips."

The smallest guns they had were .450 Powells. In addition, each had a .510 Rigby and a .600 Express. Six gunbearers carried the rifles in green canvas cases.

St. Leger and Meagher wouldn't shoot standing beasts. "Not sporting, y'know. Must bag 'em on the wing."

When I explained that I thought it more sporting to be sure of killing rather than just wounding game, St. Leger said:

"Do 'em in quickly. Elephant guns, y'know. Mustn't dispatch sitting beasts. Be like shooting sitting hares, what?"

I'd met the old codgers by appointment at their camp near Maun on the edge of the Okavango Swamp in Bechuanaland. This was in 1938. What a camp! They'd set up four large double tents of green canvas. They had deck chairs. They had bookcases. They had two tables to each tent, Aladdin lamps, cases of whiskey, and cases of squareface gin. They'd set up a Whymper tent as a kitchen and had stocked it with all sorts of canned goods. Under green tarpaulins were parked two Chevrolet pickups and a Ford flatbed.

They greeted me with grave dignity, poured me a whiskey-soda, made a few remarks about the weather, and lapsed into uneasy silence. They puffed at their pipes awhile, then Meagher said, waving his pipe at the camp:

"This sort of thing won't do, y'know."

St. Leger nodded. "Want to rough it," he said. "Not these bally conveniences. Not hunting at all. Not Africa. Silly way to shoot."

I laughed. They looked so serious. I said: "I don't like this sort of thing either. How about getting an ox-wagon outfit together and foot-slogging it about the country?"

A load seemed to drop from their shoulders. They beamed. Said Meagher:

"Sleep on the ground, what?"

"And live off the country," St. Leger added.

"Why not?" I said. "There's *hunting* and *hunting*. Too much rocking-chair shooting being done these days." Indicating the luxury of the camp with a sweep of my arm, I added: "Somebody sold you a bill of goods."

"Ha! Excellent way to put it," said Meagher. "Fast-talking chap at Pretoria outfitted us. Wouldn't stop talking, so we bought everything. Easiest way, y'know."

"Well," I said, "I'll go into Maun tomorrow and pick up a wagon outfit. It's too wet to go into the swamp. Rainy season's just ended. We'll go toward Daka, through grass, brush, and sand country. How many boys have you?"

"Twenty-eight."

"We'll leave twenty-four of them here. I'll bring a white man back from Maun to watch camp."

"Leave our gunbearers here?"

"Yes. And leave all the guns but your two .450s."

They took it on the chin like gentlemen.

Meagher got three water glasses from a cupboard. He poured them to the brim with Haig &

Haig and handed them around. "Well," he said, downing half his glass, "cheer-o."

We loaded the ox wagon with plenty of blankets, corn meal, salt, sugar, milk, liquor, oil lanterns, pots, and camping odds and ends. I chose a Bantu cook, a camp boy, an ox driver, and a *voorlooper* to lead the span. I had my own trackers, the Zulu, Ubusuku, and a Bantu named Jantje. We started northeast at dawn of the third day after my arrival. St. Leger and Meagher paced gravely beside the wagon. They thought they were fooling me, but I knew they were as excited as Boy Scouts on their first week-end camp.

I learned to love those old rascals. The wagon did about twenty miles a day, but the three of us and the trackers prowled the veldt in all directions, sometimes doing thirty miles before reaching the outspan at night.

Surprisingly, they could shoot. Steady, dogged, deliberate. They tossed a coin the first morning to see which of them would take the first shot at the first game. From then on each took his turn, the other beside him, acting as support gun.

For five days we passed through a game paradise. Not the overwhelming herds of East Africa, but small, more exciting herds of gemsbok, hartebeests, springbok, zebras, reedbuck, and duikers. Once or twice each day we spotted ostriches; and on the fifth day, beside a clear-flowing spruit, we found lion dung. That did it. The old devils got lion fever, and from that moment nothing else would do. We made our base camp right there.

It was almost two weeks before we got a lion. In

the meantime I made St. Leger and Meagher responsible for getting meat for camp.

Long before sunrise, those two happy hunters had folded their blankets, piled them neatly on the wagon bed, and were cleaning overnight oil from their rifle barrels between sips of tea from great blue enamel mugs.

I had been teaching them a bit of spooring and they became fascinated with the stories told by sign. Spooring is not a difficult art to learn if one works at it. I've seen a greenhorn become the equal of the average native tracker in a few months.

While Ubusuku, Jantje, and I stood around the fire, St. Leger and Meagher would circle camp in the dim predawn light, looking for dark, dewless animal trails through the wet grass. Down they'd get on their hands and knees looking for dung, the best identification of an animal. They kept notes like these:

"*Springbok droppings*—about the shape and size of .500 slugs.

"*Reedbuck*—sometimes like small walnuts; sometimes like .600 bullets.

"*Bushbuck*—usually an oblong waffle-looking affair, but sometimes the waffle falls into pieces."

On the day we found the first lion dung they made this entry:

"*Lion*—looks like a hairy almond the size of a lemon."

Good descriptions to a man who's seen various dungs, but not much good to anyone else.

I taught them to watch for nibbled and crushed grass, for dropped chewings; to test the moisture in hoofprints; to note whether or not the cloven hoofprints of antelope were spread wide, indicating running; and to keep their eyes open for a hundred other signs that make the veldt a book easily read—after one learns to read it. They developed fast, chiefly because they concentrated with single-minded intensity.

One midmorning Jantje grunted and pointed ahead to a group of three acacia thorn trees. A yellow-maned lion had just got to his feet and was stretching sleepily, mouth open in a wide yawn. The wind was toward us, so I said to St. Leger and Meagher:

"There's a nice trophy. About 150 yards. One of you take him."

They looked hurt. Meagher said: "Can't be done, old chap. He's standing, y'see."

"Doggone it," I said, "then walk toward him, and if he charges, shoot fast and sure."

They moved ahead side by side, their .450s across their stomachs. The lion looked at them without interest and lay down again. Not so a female that had been hidden in the shade of a second tree. She came fast, leaping low, making no sound.

I held my sights on her—just in case. But St. Leger fired, kneeling. The big lioness turned a somersault, slapped her tail a few moments, and lay quiet. The male got to his feet and moved behind a third tree. I lost sight of him for a couple of minutes, then saw him high-tailing it toward brush a half mile away.

The lioness was still. St. Leger and Meagher

looked at me. I said: "Move closer and put another slug in her. Can't ever tell."

A second shot wasn't needed. St. Leger's shot was one of the best I'd ever seen. Low in the chest, it got the lungs, heart, stomach, and liver. The old boy stood beside the dead beast, stroking his mustache with exaggerated calmness, but I noticed a trembling in his fingers.

Meagher filled and lighted his pipe. He took a few puffs, then said: "Well bowled, Topper, old boy."

Major Edward Keith-Roach poses in 1924 in the Sudan with the head of a lioness which had attacked three village boys. The boys survived by filling the mouth of the lioness with a robe and hacking it to death with a hatchet.

I'd never heard St. Leger's nickname before. It showed that beneath his composure Meagher, too, was deeply moved. Disciplined old bluffers, they were, shy as schoolboys.

Meagher got his lion about a week later. A male with a skimpy mane. Meagher said ruefully that he'd have to buy it a wig before putting the head up in his den. He got the animal with a nice quartering shot through the shoulder blade into the chest.

By this time the two old fellows, who had been overweight and in poor condition when I met them, were lean and hard. They fiddled around the veldt for the next two weeks, potting animals here and there. By the time the days got fiery hot and the grass got high and brown, they had collected one springbok, one reitbok, two buffalo, a small kudu, two zebras, and the two lions.

Then one morning in a soft spot where he had watered, a kudu bull left a clear, deep print of a hoof. It measured almost six inches from heel to points, a good one-third larger than any kudu spoor I'd ever seen. Even I got excited. This could be a record bull, one with horns sixty-seven inches measured straight. With a foot that size, he would scale over five hundred pounds, I figured. His fresh trail was well marked through the grass. I let St. Leger and Meagher take the lead. They went ahead like bird dogs.

The bull was traveling upwind. As we advanced, the grass rose from knee height to hip height and finally to our shoulders. Lions could be bad here, but I figured the old kudu wouldn't be moving so leisurely if big cats were around. Yet I was uneasy.

Then out of nowhere came an earth-jarring roar, and a male lion, blood dripping from his mouth, leaped at St. Leger. It was the first time in years I'd heard a lion really roar. St. Leger threw himself sideways, and the enraged lion missed him by inches. I shot from the hip. Meagher's gun bellowed so close to my ear that I thought for a moment I'd been hit. The lion disappeared into tall, rough-edged grass.

St. Leger was unhurt, but for once his reserve was shattered. He kept repeating: "By Jove! Oh, by Jove!" About thirty feet away we found the lion-mangled body of the kudu bull. His horns were everything we had hoped they'd be. He hadn't been dead for more than a few minutes. Blood was still oozing from awful wounds.

I went back to where we'd shot at the big cat. Both bullets had evidently hit, for a splash of blood was foamy, indicating a lung puncture, and a second puddle of blood was normal red. I said:

"While Jantje skins the kudu we'll take it easy and give the lion's wounds time to stiffen. Then Ubusuku and I'll go after him."

"It's our job," St. Leger said.

I grinned. "You'd be killed. Ubusuku'll go in on his belly. He can do it without rustling the grass. I'll follow the lion's trail. I'll be able to tell by the blood how fast he's losing strength. No—you men stay here and help Jantje with his kudu."

"It's our job," St. Leger repeated stubbornly.

"No, stay here. I don't want the reputation of having my clients killed."

They kept protesting. I said:

"Listen. A white hunter friend of mine named Van der Wall let one of his sportsmen go into brush after a wounded lion. He'd told him how foolish it was. Begged him to wait at least until the animal had time to weaken from bleeding. Explained that a wounded lion lies down at the first opportunity and that wounds stiffen if given time. He said: 'When he hears you coming, he'll stop groaning. He'll know where you are, but you won't know where he is. He won't come at you running. He'll wait until you're within feet of him.'

"That guy wouldn't listen. Said he'd come to Africa for thrills and that this was a worthwhile one. He stalked into the brush. He walked right past the lion as it lay close to the ground in heavy underbrush. The lion hit him from behind. Broke his neck, bit through his skull. Van der Wall dropped the lion on top of its victim, but that didn't do the dead man any good."

The sun was hot. Ticks were biting hard on my back. I said to Ubusuku: "Let's go over in the shade of that bush, and you can burn a couple of ticks off my back."

Ticks bury their heads deep. If you pull them off, the heads stay in the flesh and you have to dig them out with a knife. If you put the flame of a match to their backsides, they jerk their heads out in a hurry. Ubusuku got the ticks all right, and I was putting my shirt back on when Jantje yelled:

"Old men go get lion, *Baas.*"

I grunted in dismay. Ubusuku grabbed up his assagai and was gone like a flash. As I paused beside Jantje to pick up my .303, I saw Ubusuku dive headfirst into the grass. I checked the cartridges in the chamber and magazine and trotted along the lion's trail. My worry was that he would circle and, while the two men were following his spoor, would come up behind them.

The trail made a sweeping curve. Foamy blood spotted the ground grass here and there. Higher up, red blood streaks showed the beast had been hit high, probably near his rear. The blood wasn't smeared as it would have been had it been a front shot and the lion's body had rubbed against the stains in passing.

I yelled two or three times for St. Leger and Meagher to wait for me. They didn't answer. Then it happened all at once. I heard Ubusuku yell. Heard the lion cough. Heard one of the old men scream. Saw a rifle go hurtling away like a helicopter propeller. I cut through the grass to the turmoil, and my heart went sick.

St. Leger, a bloody mass, lay broken. Meagher was under the lion, and the lion, with Ubusuku's assagai sticking out like a second tail, was coughing great bubbly gobs of blood. With three shots I made a mess of that lion's head.

St. Leger had a broken collarbone, a compound fracture of the ulna, and several broken ribs. The blood on him proved to be the lion's blood. Meagher, when we got him from under the carcass, was claw-torn from shoulder to ankle. His clothes were ripped off. Terrible foreleg swipes had struck like bolts of lightning. Had the lion been an inch closer when he struck, he'd have disemboweled Meagher.

Well, we got Meagher's bleeding stopped after a while, and he cursed as I poured iodine in his wounds. I took the first-aid kit over to St. Leger and bandaged him as well as possible. It took seven days to get the old gentlemen to Maun, where a private plane took them to Livingstone. Two weeks later I visited them in the hospital. As I walked into their room I heard Meagher calling St. Leger a brittle-boned old female. St. Leger grinned at me and said:

"Toss a coin, will you, old chap? Tails I get that bunged-up lion's head and Scar-bottom over there gets the kudu."

I tossed a coin.

It came down tails.

The natives often lived in fear of marauding lions. The killing of this one in Central Africa in 1926 was cause for great rejoicing.

8

MORE BABOONS

I FIRST SAW THE FARM when I was hunting baboons in the Magaliesbergen. It was early morning, and I'd been clambering along the ridge of *kopjes* for more than three hours, stopping to watch the sun lift from the darkness and turn the somber ground-mists into a violet haze all shot with flashes of pearl and silver; to watch the dew-moist rocks of the lower slopes change under the warming morn light from black to brown, to rusted red.

Suddenly the mists were gone and the tawny veldt, dotted with green bushes and black wait-a-bit thorn trees, shimmered and quivered in the beginnings of the heat mirage. As the sun's rays grew more fiery, a breeze rustled the warming air strata and the trees and bushes began a weird dance, shifting about, floating a few feet off the ground, and changing their shapes like reflections seen in riffled waters.

A four-hundred-pound hartebeest walked from a shadow into the heat haze and instantly grew larger than an elephant. He lifted slowly, floated, expanded, and shrank.

Abruptly the veldt gave birth to a twin that hung in the sky upside down; grass and bushes and trees and hartebeests, all exact duplicates of their prototypes. The mirage faded. And the veldt, weary of fantasy, was hot and quiet and sleepy.

The farm lay directly below me, snuggling close to the feet of the *kopje*. The house was white and low and seemed small under its thick, weathered-grass thatch. The barn had walls of woven reeds beneath a flat roof of corrugated galvanized iron. A vine-covered privy was enclosed on three sides by a hedge of prickly pear.

It was a lazy farm, for the sun was getting high and no white folks were about. I focused my field glasses on the back door of the house. It was a Dutch door, and the top half was open. A ragged male ostrich came around the corner, stepping high. He stuck his head through the open door. There was a flurry of white cloth as a dish towel slapped him in the face. He danced angrily away, his wings half spread. A Zulu woman thrust her head into the open and screamed, "*Voetsak* (go away)!"

Three yellow cows came out of the barn and stood patiently while being milked by a young Kaffir who wore nothing but dark shorts and a woman's red straw hat. He carried the milk bucket to the back door. A black hand reached out and took it. The boy, like the ostrich, put his head through the doorway and leaped back as the white towel knocked his hat from his head. He put his hat back on, went into the barn, came out with a long-handled, long-lashed ox whip, and shouting

"Eeyak!" cracked it over the backs of the cows. He drove them into a fenced field and shut the gate. Then he placed his whip on the ground, stretched himself on his back, crossed his feet, placed his hat over his face, and lay quiet.

Beyond the house the trees of a small orange orchard reflected golden flashes from glistening leaves. Two American mules grazed among several oxen beside a wide, shallow creek. Three baboon poles, each with its little board seat on top, stood halfway between the house and the barn. At the base of each a chained baboon sat beside his "doghouse."

A dusty road wound from the barn, crossed the creek over a planked bridge, and entered a grove of *moepel,* wild fig, and medlar trees. A gray ape about one eighth the size of a baboon walked out of the grove and sat in the road. He scratched his sides for a while, then got up and walked back into the shadows.

I became possessed by an eerie impression that I had known these scenes before. I felt as though "ghost-like I paced round the haunts of my childhood." Fantastic, of course, for I had been born in Illinois and reared in Michigan. Yet everything seemed familiar, even the ape and the ostrich.

A few minutes after I had begun the ten-mile trudge back to my tent in the *kloof* beside the *kopje* where I hunted baboons, I paused and looked back. Smoke from the kitchen chimney clung to the thatch as if loath to leave. I said to myself: "Someday I'll come back and buy that farm."

I did. But not until after three years of lonely,

roadless treks through Rhodesia, German Southwest Africa, the Congo, Tanganyika, Kenya, and the waterless, hellhole country north of the Oaso Nyiro. Weary of killing at last, Ubusuku and I headed south. In Bulawayo we picked up bank drafts from the Berlin Zoological Gardens and museums in the south of Europe—drafts that had been piling up for two years. Ubusuku went home to Natal to buy some wives and to "keep them filled with children." I bought a salted horse and headed for the Magaliesbergen—and the farm.

Rose, the owner, sold me everything—the land, the animals, the furniture, the sunrises and sunsets, the purple of night, the crying of *nacht* apes in the grove, the reflection of candlelight on the polished ebony-black mud-and-dung floor, the voiceless yearnings, the welling poems for which there can never be words, and the peace of timeless waiting that comes to lonely men in Africa.

I sat alone on the *stoep* until long after the sun had set and the stars had come out to hang on silver threads in the moonless sky—like luminescent spiders. Then I went into the house and sat for a while in the good dark.

At last a Kaffir came from the barn, lighted candles, and made coffee; not the effeminate stuff from patented coffee makers, but the rich, dark brown, bitter, satisfying brew of coffee boiled in a two-quart blue enamel pot; a pot black with smoke; a pot never washed. He brought a tin of berry jam, a platter of plump white sea biscuits, and a small Gorgonzola cheese.

An impulsive breeze slipping through the open

top of the front door stirred the candle flames and the corner shadows as it passed on its way to the open door at the back.

I set the empty coffee cup down and said to the waiting Kaffir: "What's your name?"

"Jim, *Baas.*"

"Okay, Jim. Go to bed."

He grinned and stepped into the shadows. His voice came out of the darkness: *"Shlala gaashly, Baas."*

"Hamba gaashly, Jim."

In the morning I stood on the packed-earth floor of the front stoep and watched the sun rise above the orange trees. The ragged ostrich came out of the orchard, passed around the house toward the back. I hurried into the kitchen, grabbed up a towel, and as he put his head inside I flipped it in his face. He danced back huffily. I laughed aloud. Everything was as I had dreamed it would be. I threw the ostrich a loaf of bread.

I looked up at the *kopje.* A file of baboons was silhouetted along the ridge where I'd stood a thousand toilsome treks ago. My baboons—my *kopje!*

There had been little change. The same Kaffir milked three yellow cows beside the barn. His hat now was a battered felt. Only two baboons were chained to the posts in the yard: an old dog baboon and a three-quarter-grown female. The mules were there, and the oxen. I walked into the orchard and counted the orange trees—an even hundred. Off by itself grew a *naarjie* (tangerine) tree; too plebeian to associate with the aristocratic oranges.

In a small pond, gunny sacks filled with tobacco leaves were soaking; the wet leaves to be twisted someday into ropes, dried, and thus become the vilest pipe tobacco known to man.

I strolled again to the back of the house and stopped in alarm. The male baboon lay on his side, a six-month-old Kaffir baby in his arms. I backed out of sight, hurried around the house, through the front door, picked up a rifle and, standing well back from the open kitchen door, placed the butt against my shoulder.

I lowered the gun as Jim's wife, a girl with thighs like tree trunks, brought a large, empty box and placed it on the ground close to the baboon. She took off her blanket, folded it, placed it in the box, took the baby from the baboon, and laid it on the blanket. The baboon got into the box and once again wrapped his arms about the child. The black woman nodded as if satisfied and walked away.

I put my rifle down and called Jim. I was trembling with anger when he showed up. I said: "Damn it, Jim, are you crazy? "

Jim looked bewildered. *"B-Baas?"* he stammered

"Go get that baby from the baboon. Hurry!"

"Ja, Baas," Jim said, and, turning, yelled a string of Zulu words at his wife. She ran to the box, her big breasts bouncing, picked up the baby, and moved beyond the limit of the baboon's chain. Then she stared at me with frightened eyes.

I said: "Jim, turn that baboon loose. Chase him up to his pals on the *kopje*. Make quick, Jim."

"Baas, please...."

I picked up the rifle and said: "Turn him loose or I'll kill him."

Sullenly Jim undid the baboon's collar. The baboon just sat.

I said: "Chase him, damn it! Chase him toward the *kopje.*"

Jim waved his arms and yelled. The baboon opened his mouth as if yawning, then shuffled over to the privy, climbed up the vines, and squatted on the roof.

"He is a good baboon, *Baas,*" Jim said. "He is just like a minister. He cannot go to the *kopje*. The wild baboons will kill him."

"Kill him? Why?"

"Because he has the man-stink, *Baas.*"

I thought a moment, then said: "Okay. He can stay here, but don't ever let that baby near him again. If you do, you can get the hell back to Zululand."

When Jim had gone, I sat in a chair and listened to my heart pound. After a while I went outside. The baboon was again on his chain.

During the next few days Jim helped me get acquainted with my farm. His wife's name was Selina. The baby was Mafuta (the Fat One). The Kaffir who milked the cows was a Basuto boy called Charlie. The old male baboon was Predikant (Preacher). The female baboon was Tante (Auntie). The ostrich was Oscar. There were ducks and ducklings, hens and chicks. There was a lonely old sow that had gone half wild and lived in the rushes along the creek.

The fourteen long-horned oxen were all named

Mountain with a prefix denoting the animal's color. They were named in Boer Dutch, of course. There was Rooiberg (Red Mountain), Swartberg (Black Mountain), Witberg (White Mountain), and on through blue, brown, gray, roan, and variegated hues.

Jim and I walked over the farm from boundary to boundary. One line was the ridge of the *kopje*. The opposite line crossed level veldt one thousand yards below the house. Our only crop was oranges, and there weren't enough of them to do much more than pay the wages of the natives.

We grew our own vegetables and tobacco. We had milk. There was meat for the shooting—hartebeest, duikerbok, *lagavaan* (large water lizards), and water rats. Selina made jams and jellies from wild figs, wild dates, wild peaches, and large, luscious berries.

The baboons were mine, as were the rock hares and the rabbits, the leopards, pythons, and the cool, sweet pools of the *kloofs;* as were the apes in the grove, the antelope in the fields, the secretary birds that nested in the thorn-tree tops, and the birds that flitted about like bright jewels in the orchard.

It was a lazy, lazy farm. Selina, Jim, and Charlie did all the work. I wrote articles about animals and hunting when in the mood, which was seldom. I spent a lot of time watching the two baboons petting and cuddling the ducklings and chicks that came within reach; watching them scrape up little piles of pebbles so they'd be handy to throw at Charlie when he passed; watching them torment the silly hens.

Alexander Lake 163

Baboon up a tree in Malawi, doubtless planning some mischief.

Photo: Carol Resnick

Every morning Tante and Predikant would leave a few mealie (corn) kernels from their breakfast, then pretend to sleep. The hens, who never seemed to learn better, would approach haltingly, stopping every step or two to look at the baboons, first with one eye, then the other. The baboons, smiling smugly, watched through slitted eyelids. The hens pecked at the first few kernels nervously, then, forgetting their vigilance, would begin eating greedily. The next instant, as two lionlike roars shook the morning, the hens, like leaves in a whirlwind, would be flapping off every which way in squawking hysteria. The baboons loved it.

Predikant and Tante were male and female. They lived side by side; sometimes they sat atop their poles at the same time. Yet they ignored each other entirely. It may be that Tante had no sex urge. But Predikant did. He never tried to hide his fiendish desires when the wild sow wandered by.

One day I said to Jim: "It would be nice to have a little baboon about the place. Let's fasten Predikant and Tante to the same pole and see what happens."

"It has been tried, *Baas*. Nothing happens."

"Well, let's try again. The wild baboons are mating on the *kopje*. Maybe they'll give Tante ideas. Predikant seems to have ideas already."

"He has no ideas for Tante. *Baas*, nor for any baboon. He thinks only of the pig." Jim spat disgustedly.

He was right. We kept Predikant chained to Tante's pole for over a month. He didn't even bother to pick fleas off her.

Predikant missed Mafuta, Jim's baby. Every time Selina came to the door of her shack, the baboon stared eagerly. If Selina carried the baby past him, he would rock on his feet and strain at his chain. Once he got loose and they found him standing, peering through the shack's one window.

The wild baboons played and barked on the *kopje,* sometimes within three hundred yards of the house. Predikant turned his back on them. Tante watched them without interest.

Captive baboons are water. Wild baboons are whiskey.

I began spending more and more time with the wild ones. They soon learned I was trying to be friendly and would eat the dried mealies I strewed about as I walked close to the troop. One day I found some stale popcorn in the pantry. I dropped it with the mealies, and the baboons were delighted. I sent Jim to Pretoria for one hundred pounds of it and spent the evenings popping corn in a covered frying pan.

Whenever I had popcorn with me the younger baboons followed me like kids following an ice wagon. Sometimes when I brought none and they realized there'd be no treat that day, they acted rudely. They'd rush at me with arms held out stiffly, stopping suddenly to jump up down and gibber at me. Then they'd turn their backs and make faces at me from between their legs.

As I said before, it was a lazy farm and I was lazy, too, except when footslogging over hill and valley with rifle or camera. Here was my opportunity to become an authority on the chacma baboon—a good excuse to get out of work. For weeks I practically lived with the fascinating rogues.

One morning I noticed a strange quietness among the three hundred or more baboons in the troop I had been observing. Usually, at that time of day, the baboons were noisily active among the rocks, along the *krans*, and in the dense brush of the *kloof*.

I had been standing at the base of the *kopje* for almost an hour watching some playing youngsters through my field glasses. The abrupt cessation of barks and roars on the hillside startled me, and when out of the silence a single voice rose in a despairing wail, I felt an actual chill flicker on the back of my neck.

The wail became a long, drawn-out moan and rose again to a sort of agonizing shriek. Then I saw something I've never seen baboons do before. Males from every part of the *kopje* began moving *silently* toward the outcry. I sensed that it was a female voicing the unbearable distress. So human, so urgent was her appeal that without realizing it I, too, moved toward her, my hand on the revolver at my side.

I stopped after a few paces, for the silence of those converging males was ominous. I'd watched this troop approach threatening pythons, leopards, and men many times, but always before it had been with roars, barks, shrieks, and discordant challenges.

I looked toward where, until the wailing began, sentries had been posted in dead trees and on top of rocks. All had joined the horde of advancing males. Females and youngsters had vanished.

I had been studying these baboons for more than fourteen weeks and thought I had learned to recognize the types of danger threatening them by the quality of their hullabaloo. This time I couldn't even guess at the peril.

The wailing stopped as the males concentrated near a rock outcropping halfway up the slope. They sat motionless, not even turning their heads. I watched them until the heat from my face misted my field glasses. As I wiped the lenses I became aware of the chief troop leader emerging from behind a boulder less than thirty feet from me. He sat down facing me, his arms dangling, and stared over my head. My hand started toward my revolver, but something in his attitude restrained me. Then from behind that same boulder five more troop leaders moved into the open and seated themselves in a row a few feet behind their chief. They, too, looked past me into the distance.

This situation was not only beyond my experience, but it was beyond anything I had ever imagined. The old "headman" was a fighting baboon, of which there is at least one in every troop. Not long before, I had seen him kill a boar hound by holding it by the ears and tearing out its bowels with his back hands. I had watched him and two other males destroy a leopard. Now there he sat motionless, seeing me from the corners of his eyes, but not looking directly at me.

I didn't know what to do. I felt the slight breeze cool the nervous sweat on my forehead and upper lip. My revolver was useless against so many. Afraid to take my eyes off them, I moved backward slowly, a few inches at a step.

Then the baboon chief looked at me. Usually it's impossible to get a baboon to look you in the eyes, but this big 150-pounder was staring straight into mine. His eyes were yellow, with red high lights. In them was no anger, no excitement—just a strange *straining,* as if he were desperately trying to break through the darkness between his mind and mine.

I said softly, "My God!" Sweat streamed down my sides. I backed another few inches, and he shifted his eyes to a point over my shoulder.

Another wail rose shrill on the *kopje.* All six of the baboons got to their feet and moved directly up the slope. They didn't look back, but *I knew* they wanted me to follow them.

I did. My mind was in a conflict of curiosity, wonder, unbelief, and fear. I wanted to turn and run, yet I seemed impelled to see this thing through.

As I rounded the huge outcropping, the ring of males sitting near it moved back. The six leaders walked a little way, then grouped themselves on their buttocks and stared past me. The female who had been wailing backed away several yards, sat down, and was quiet.

Almost at my feet a baby baboon writhed and twisted on the ground. I wanted to pick it up—to do something for it—but I didn't dare. To frighten or even touch a baby baboon is to ask every male in the troop down upon you in raging anger. Some men and many dogs have been torn to shreds for such temerity.

I looked at the ring of silent males. I looked at the six huddled leaders. None seemed to know I was there. I glanced at the baby's mother. She, too, stared far off.

As a game hunter, I had faced peril many times. I knew what fear was and how I reacted to it. But this conflict within me between the urge to help the baby baboon and the drive to get away as fast as I could was something new. When a lion attacks, you stop him with a bullet—or you don't. Either way, it's between you and the lion. But this situation, in which there was nothing I could do to help myself, seemed fantastically hopeless.

I took a tentative step toward the little sufferer, then glanced at the baboons. They didn't even shift their gazes. I took another step and stopped again. Still no movement. I looked at the mother. Her fangs were bared, but she wasn't looking at me. I moved to within a yard of the little fellow and saw the cause of its desperate sickness. A tiny pile of mealie kernels, stained a light green with ant poison, lay near him. Two or three half-chewed kernels were in the foam around his lips.

I knew at once what had happened. Charlie, the boy in charge of my cows, had poisoned the mealies and left them on the hillside. He hated baboons. And they hated him. Poisoned mealies do not tempt adult baboons, but babies have to learn.

Fear vanished in a rush of anger, and I knelt beside the gasping youngster. My canteen was filled with bitter-strong coffee. I opened the baby's mouth and poured coffee down his throat. He struggled weakly. His mother made a hoarse but subdued squawk. I squeezed the baby's belly, and foul, yellow curds gushed from his mouth. I poured more coffee into him. He lay still, and I thought he was dead. He gasped and moved. More coffee. He lay panting. I watched, realizing that if he died I'd probably die too. Spasms shook him, but they came farther and farther apart. He began making soft whimpering noises. The mother moved toward me. I backed away. With a rush she gathered up her baby and, holding him in one arm, jolted away on three legs.

My sweat held that unforgettable stink that comes from fear. There was weakness in my legs, and I thought I'd fall. With my foot I crushed the poisoned kernels into the ground, then looked up to see the baboons ambling away about their business. By the time I'd reached the *kopje's* foot they were once again barking and "waughing" all over the hill.

I soon got over my fright, but I've never forgotten the intense "yearning" in the eyes of that baboon leader. I've known ever since that the gray baboon is closer to the fringe of human thought than most persons can bring themselves to believe.

We were friends—those "dog-faced mountain men" and I. We remained friends until I sold the farm and once again, with Ubusuku, went a-hunting.

9

BUFFALO

YOU'RE GOING after African buffalo. You've read a lot about them and no doubt you're excited over the possibility of some thrilling encounters. Well, calm down. Chances are about five thousand to one against your meeting up with one of those much-publicized, murderously minded bulls. What you're more likely to see are the rapidly disappearing hind ends of hundreds of shy, apprehensive herds.

Scores of professionals have hunted buffalo for years without ever having had to do battle with a rogue. However, if you should have the good (or bad) luck to meet one, you've met a dangerous character. Unless you know something about his behavior habits, you may find yourself engaged in one of the most even-up man-versus-animal contests in Africa. On the other hand, if you have an unusual type of courage and an understanding of what makes a buffalo tick, you can make even the meanest would-be killer about as futile as a pansy.

Buffalo in a herd are so afraid of men that they take off at the first indication that a human is near.

The potentially dangerous animals are lone bulls, and cows shut off from their calves.

A buffalo is smart. No mistake about that. But he's not nearly so smart as many hunting yarns would have you believe. A buffalo's reactions to stimuli are almost always the same. He usually runs from the first shot, wounded or not. Sometimes he'll circle wide and come back looking for trouble. Even then, if you leave him alone, he's apt to decide to skip it and take off. A second shot, however, may really get his dander up. How mad he gets depends upon where the bullet hits him.

If the wound is very painful, he'll likely charge, for severe pain drives him to such rage that he loses all good sense. On the other hand, if it's a slug through the guts or through the flesh, the beast is more apt to wheel snorting downwind and disappear as fast as four good legs will take him.

If he does that, you've made an enemy. Watch out. You can almost bet he'll circle until he comes across his own spoor. Then he'll pick a spot ten or twelve yards away, lie down, and remain motionless, sometimes for hours, sometimes for days. About the only way of knowing he's alive is to watch for the twitching of his nose and ears, for day and night he sniffs the breeze and listens for approaching danger.

Sometimes he'll choose to lurk in heavy brush. But don't depend on that. He's just as apt to lie down in the open against a dark background, with maybe a single small bush in front of him to break his outline. In either place he's invisible to the untrained eye so long as he doesn't move.

I've heard hunters say that the buffalo will always hide on the side of the spoor from which he approached it. This is not true. He crosses his trail and hides just as often as not. *And he's not waiting for the guy who wounded him.* He's waiting there because his instincts tell him it's the safest place for him. He lies as quietly as possible to give his stiffening wounds a chance to heal and to keep from being spotted by an enemy. He lies close to the trail because he senses that in his condition, his charge, if he has to make one, must be lightning-fast.

About half the time when a hunter passes the buffalo's hiding place the beast lets the man go on in blissful ignorance of the fact that death was only feet away. Other times he comes out so abruptly that his victim is flying through the air like a whirling swastika before knowing what hit him. If the victim moves after he hits the ground, the buffalo will either toss him again or trample him.

Buffalo herds never charge a human, but sometimes a human will get in the way of a stampede. Here's the way you should handle it: Lie down until the herd gets within a hundred yards, then jump to your feet and stand waving your arms gently. Don't overdo it, for some animal brushing past may take fright and swipe at you with his horns.

On the shores of Lake Kivu in the Congo, Commander Attilio Gatti, the Italian explorer, once got caught in a stampede of three hundred buffalo. They came thundering. Gatti screamed, shouted, and waved his coat and hat wildly. The herd split and passed on each side of him, some within inches. Gatti got away with it, but he'd have been safer had he stood still. His good angel saved him, for his violent gymnastics might have startled one of the passing animals into making a sweep at him.

Buffalo can make it tough on a man, but there are ways for a man to make it tough on the buff. One is to use the tactics of the bull ring. Take a blanket, and just before the charging animal lowers his head for the thrust, hold the blanket in front of you and step quietly sideways. The buffalo will go after the blanket. You could, if you wanted, do a bullfighter's simple Veronica and lead the buffalo into a series of futile attacks.

In other words, you can handle a buffalo just as the matador handles a bull. I've seen it done. Not by a white man, but by a Hottentot. He'd aggravate a buffalo bull until it charged, flip out his blanket, and step barely clear. As the beast hit the blanket, the Hottentot would drop the blanket neatly over its head. Then he'd stick two, sometimes three, spears into the buffalo and take off like an antelope. The bull, shaking off the blanket, would toss it, trample it, snort at it, work it over—and drop dead.

A buffalo won't toss or trample a dead man he hasn't killed himself. Up in the Lake Edward district of Uganda many natives are adept at playing dead. They start downwind from a herd, work close, pick out the beast they want, and let fly at it with two or three poisoned arrows. Then down they flop in the grass, lying limp and barely breathing. They dare not run because it's open country, and even the fastest native can't outrun an angry buffalo.

Usually the wounded beast fusses and fumes because of the sting of the arrows but makes no attempt to discover the hunter. Sometimes, however, he scents or hears the man and comes at him a-bellowing. The native sometimes is actually turned over by the animal's forefeet as he plows to a stop. Puzzled, the buffalo puts his nose against the body and snorts and grumbles. He walks away, turns suddenly, and eyes the "corpse." Sometimes he comes back and sniffs and snorts some more. Finally the poison gets to him. He moves away, collapses, groans, and dies.

There's one weakness of the buffalo that even some of the oldest professionals find hard to believe. I discovered it by accident, and the knowledge came in handy two or three times in later years. It's this: *A good hard smash on the tip of a buffalo's nose takes all the fight out of him.*

Back in 1921 as I was leaving Bulawayo for a quick trip to the Sabi River, a twenty-two-year-old Yorkshire lad named Frankie Manley begged me to take him along. He told me he'd bummed his way from England to photograph game. He had two battered second-hand cameras and a pitifully meager supply of film. He had no money and offered to work his way.

"Look, I'll be your white Kaffir," he said. "I'll work myself thin if you'll only take me along."

He was so eager that he shook. What could I do? "Okay," I said.

Frankie proved to be the goosiest man I've ever

heard of. If touched anywhere, back or front, between his neck and feet, he'd yell like a banshee and either strike or kick anything in front of him. We weren't out of Bulawayo an hour when Jomo, my ox driver, accidentally poked Frankie in the back with the tip of the long ox whip. Frankie was walking behind a kitchen boy named Jappie. With a yell that tangled the sixteen oxen in their yoke straps Frankie kicked Jappie, knocking him flat. Then he turned right about in mid-jump and, with head down, began belting the empty air with both fists.

On the wagon was a small coop containing fourteen hens. One morning a chicken got out and with a squawk flew blindly against the back of Frankie's knees. So help me, I thought a hyena had been run over by the wagon.

Fortunately there was no one near the kid, for he made five or six jumps, kicking out with all his might at each jump.

None of the Kaffirs would go within fifty feet of Frankie. Those kicks were dangerous. Frankie weighed close to 190 pounds.

One day just before noon we came across a herd of nine buffalo drinking from a shallow stream. Frankie wanted a picture, so I motioned one of the boys to carry my rifle and walked unarmed toward the peaceful herd with Frankie. I'd spun many a yarn to him, and he knew how the Uganda natives played dead in a pinch.

We got up close, and Frankie got a couple of pictures. The Kaffir with the rifle was close at my heels. The herd seemed as inoffensive as a herd of

Jerseys. Then, without warning, a bull lifted his head, bellowed, and charged across the narrow stream—straight at Frankie. I whirled for my rifle. Kaffir and rifle were one hundred yards away and going all out. I headed for a small tree. Frankie stumbled and fell flat.

He lay so still I thought he'd been knocked out. That bull stopped so fast he sat down, his braced forefeet not six inches from Frankie's heels.

I was stumped. No gun. No idea what to do.

The bull shook his head until his ears flapped, then placed his muzzle against the back of Frankie's thighs—and snorted.

Frankie came off the ground screaming like a V-2 rocket. He whirled and kicked that buffalo smack between the nostrils. The bull, nose close to the ground, snorted spurts of sand into the air, all the while backing toward the river. But when he saw Frankie galloping toward my tree, he took out after him. I went up the tree with Frankie right behind me. It was a precarious perch. The tree swayed perilously under our weight. But up we stayed for almost an hour while the bull, making the damnedest noises, circled the trunk. Round and round he'd go, stop downwind, stick his nose out straight, sniff and blow, then start his merry-go-round again.

Finally he gave up and went off at a trot.

I found my rifle choked with dirt. I never again saw that gunbearer.

The African buffalo is a particularly nasty customer in high grass, reeds, or brush. If he's in the prime of life, he'll weigh around sixteen hundred pounds and his horn spread will vary from thirty-six to fifty-four inches. The thing that makes him most dangerous to humans is the number of heavy-caliber bullets he can take and still keep on fighting.

I once saw three sportsmen pour four .450 slugs and one .510 into the side of a five-year-old bull. He'd been trotting broadside to the hunters about eighty yards away. When the fifth bullet hit, he turned toward the shooters and broke into a raging gallop, grunting with each jump. Two of the men fell pants-seat over kettle as they bumped each other in their rush to get away. The third ran a few steps, stopped, dropped to a knee, put gun to shoulder, but held fire until the beast was within twenty yards.

Thirty yards farther back, I cut loose with my .303 at the same instant. Both bullets took the bull at the base of the throat. He turned a somersault, coming to rest on his belly, neck stretched out, all four legs doubled under him. With all that lead in him, he wasn't quite dead, for as we stepped near he gave a low, moaning bellow—and died.

"Shock" doesn't mean a thing to a buffalo. Either you get a vital spot, or you don't get your trophy without a battle. A head shot doesn't pay off against a buffalo coming head on. He comes nose up, watching you every second. He's so tough that even a broken shoulder won't stop his forward rush until the useless leg swings and trips him.

I'm a believer in the .303, .30/.06, .270, or similar calibers for all game. Yet I've sometimes wished I'd been carrying a piece of artillery when looking up the slime-dripping nostrils of a red-eyed, charging, gray-black buff.

A buffalo's color tells quite a story. Young, virile bulls are gray-black and hairy. Animals less than two and a half years old are sort of a sorrel. Old, half-deaf, half-blind animals are light gray, with little hair and worn or broken horn tips. The old bulls are still fast on their feet, but there's no excuse for tangling with them, because any man who isn't bumble-footed can sneak up on them. Most oldsters would have a hard time seeing you if they wore bifocals, and they'd probably not hear you if they carried ear trumpets. Don't mess with the old gray devils. Slip up close and do them in. One slug in the temple back of the eye will do it. So will a bullet through the jugular. The heart shot is good, but it takes time to be fatal—maybe one minute, maybe two.

In big-game hunting there seems to be a connection between the absurd and the tragic. I know the stories of many men killed by animals, and in almost every case death was preceded by some ludicrous or farcical incident. In the cases of the only two men I've seen gored by buffalo, everyone except the victims was laughing seconds before tragedy struck.

In July 1922, I made a trip from Luanda with a Portuguese official named Avila. I never did know exactly what he was up to, but when we got to where the Zambezi River leaves Angola and enters Northern Rhodesia, he and his natives began doing some hectic surveying. I assumed he was trying to clear up some border dispute. He'd brought several rifles with him, among them a brand-new .450 double-barreled H. & H. The rifle had never been shot and, because it had been stored on the damp coast, had been literally buried in Vaseline. The barrels were plugged with it.

Among Avila's natives was a half-caste Mbunda called Mao. He wasn't a bad sort, but inclined to be nosy and cheeky. One evening Avila told him to get out the H. & H. and clean it well.

Next morning when the sun began to get hot an old one-horned bull buffalo sauntered to a *moyela* tree about seventy-five yards from camp and lay down for his long midday nap. Avila was gone with his survey gang. I was typing an article on my old Yost typewriter. The machine was full of sand and sounded like a bunch of chirping beetles. Jim, my personal kitchen boy, tapped me on the shoulder and said:

"Mao take gun."

I looked up just in time to see the half-caste push a shell into one of the chambers of Avila's .450. I yelled, for it's unheard of for a native to use a white man's gun without permission. Mao paid no attention and ran toward the buffalo. I grabbed my rifle and ran after him. He was about thirty-five yards from the bull when it started to get to its feet.

Mao took quick aim and fired.

The report sounded like a World War I whiz-bang. Mao's heels came up, his shoulders went down. The back of his head hit the ground—hard. The muzzle of the .450 pointed to the zenith for an instant, then arrowed away like a thrown spear.

The buffalo trotted away, unharmed.

Mao staggered to his feet, chittering like a frightened hyrax, his dark skin paled to the color of dirty dough. Blood ran from his mouth and nose. One eye was swelling fast. He said quaveringly: "Forgot him grease in barrel."

The half-caste's ego had been punctured like a blown-out tire, and the camp boys rolled on the ground with laughter. I laughed too.

Someone shrieked. I turned and saw the bull coming like a locomotive. I had time for just one snap shot from the hip before the brute dodged me, heading for Mao. Mao dropped to his knees as if in prayer. The bull hit him low—and tossed him high. Mao crashed to the ground. I got the beast through the temple, but not before he'd rammed that single horn through Mao's neck. A hurried examination showed that the toss had killed Mao, not the horn.

The day was unusually hot, so we buried Mao when Avila returned to camp for his afternoon tea.

In November 1939, a second goring incident happened. I was busy doing nothing in Johannesburg. One afternoon a British Government official asked me to guide a Professor Lennert Cashmore to the Barotse country of northwestern Rhodesia. I was told he was an entomologist with a yen to study African insects. If the trip had been to any other part of the continent, I'd have turned it down. But in all Africa, the Barotse district is my favorite hunting spot.

Put the point of a compass on the town of Sekoski and describe a circle with a radius of three hundred miles. Within that circumference you have the finest hunting in the world. There's everything. Elephants, lions, leopards, hippos, crocodiles, rhinos, antelope, and buffalo. There's fishing such as Izaak Walton never dreamed of; wild ducks, geese, and bustards—tastier than turkey. You have scenery: grassy plains, deserts, marshes, sponge flats, lovely hidden valleys, hills, forests, and bush. You'll find grass ten feet high and parklike areas where the grass looks like the close-mowed lawns of Old England.

You have heat. And you have cooling breezes when the winds blow across the water-filled lowlands after the rains. Your circle takes in parts of Northern Rhodesia, Angola, Bechuanaland, and Damaraland. Be sure you've made arrrangements to go back and forth among the four countries. All four governments are co-operative, and they won't take your shirt to pay for game licenses.

We were in open brush country along the Lunga River. It was midmorning and hot, for there'd been no rain yet. Cashmore and I had been sitting in the shade of a group of thorn trees watching a herd of more than one hundred buffalo plod along an old trail in single file. They were heading for their siesta among heavy brush farther toward the river.

About thirty yards in front of us was a bush, possibly three feet high. Suddenly the black stern of a buffalo lifted above and beyond it as an old cow got up on her feet. She stepped into the open, twisted her tail, stretched, and let out a subdued bellow that sounded like a yawn.

Cashmore said, "Watch out!" and started up a thorn tree like a squirrel. He wasn't four feet off the ground before his clothing got so tangled in the thorns that he couldn't move. He began to yell.

The cow jumped as if a bee had got under her tail. She ran maybe fifty feet, turned, and walked hesitatingly toward us. She looked a bit insulted and intensely curious. Then she charged me. I shot her just below the horns. She grunted and came on at a canter. I dodged behind Cashmore's tree. The cow slid to a stop beside Cashmore, hooked a horn into his dangling leg, and then fell dead.

I got Cashmore down by cutting off the branches that were holding him. He was bleeding profusely. I cut his clothes off, and with water from my canteen washed the nasty hole on the side of his thigh. When I began bandaging the wound I discovered that his hip was broken. Eighteen months later he was still on crutches.

Buffalo are almost everywhere in Africa. I've shot them in Ovamboland, Angola, Congo, Rhodesia, Tanganyika, Kenya, Ethiopia, Somaliland, and in the Camaroons. They're found in marsh and in swamp country, open brush and on treeless plains. Hunting them is about the same everywhere except in bogs and marshes, where heavy going slows the hunter to a walk but where buffalo get over the ground almost as fast as anywhere else.

While buffalo fear man and will run from him, they don't recognize him as a man. It's the guy's scent that upsets them—and the way he approaches them. Most novices stalk buffalo by creeping, crawling, popping up and down in grass, dodging behind bushes, and generally emulating the red Indians of Cooper's *Leatherstocking Tales*.

No wonder the beasts run. Nothing else, not even a lion, approaches them with such queer goings on.

A professional hunter walks toward the herd. He goes slowly, without noise and without talking. If the herd shows nervousness, the hunter stops long enough to let the brutes calm down, then moves forward again. Most African animals will let an erect man come within sixty yards or so before deciding that discretion is the better part of valor. That goes for antelope, lions, rhinos, and hippos. But not for the leopard.

If the professional is after a buffalo head, he pauses at about one hundred yards and through his field glasses selects the one he wants. The horns must be large, with a wide spread and well matched. The more perfect the curve, the better the price. Once his animal is selected, he works to a point where he can get in his favorite shot. Some let drive at the small of the back just forward of the hips. Others choose a spot low in the chest, a handbreadth or more behind the foreleg—heart! They don't try any head shots, of course. They'd spoil the trophy.

They let the second aimed shot off in about three seconds. It takes that long to work the bolt and line the sights. It also takes the buffalo that long to get over the shock of the first bullet if it doesn't drop him. Most professionals place the second bullet in the chest or in the shoulder.

No professional takes the hard way to shoot an animal. He lies prone if grass isn't too high. He kneels, elbow on knee, as second choice. If he can

The African buffalo is not inclined to forgive and forget.

lay the barrel alongside a tree trunk, he'll do that. If forced to shoot standing without support, he doesn't take a trapshooter's fancy stance. His left hand will be at the point of balance, not stretched out almost full length. His left elbow is against his short ribs. The rifle rests solidly in his palm. He pulls the butt against his shoulder with the left hand, leaving the right hand and arm free to work the bolt. He doesn't take the butt from his shoulder. He moves his chin just enough to get it away from the pulled-back bolt.

If the buffalo charges, the professional keeps on shooting *aimed shots* every three seconds so long as the beast's nose is up. When the animal drops his head for a thrust, the hunter skips aside. The faster the buffalo comes, the better, for a fast charge carries the animal past far enough to let the hunter be set for another shot when the beast turns.

Someday someone's going to make a lot of money with buffalo because, contrary to popular belief, the buffalo is easily tamed. He makes a willing work animal and can pull twice the load of an ox.

In areas where buffalo are not shot at, they sometimes become a nuisance to farmers. They get into fields and even graze close to houses and barns. Among the Ovampo of Southwest Africa and the natives of southwestern Ethiopia, buffalo are sometimes used as riding oxen. The trick is to catch them young, treat them kindly, and train them patiently.

A buffalo steer is as good eating as a Hereford. That's one reason I believe, as many old-timers do, that cowboys will someday ride herd on beef buffalo in Africa just as they do on cattle in Texas.

Lions, too, think buffalo make good eating. But I don't believe the lion was ever born that had enough foolhardiness to attack a buffalo by himself. A dead lion and a dead buffalo have frequently been found lying side by side, which gives rise to belief that lone lions do sometimes attack. Three or four times I've run across such carcasses, but in each case the spoor around the scene of battle showed that the lion had had help. In one case two lions had jumped the buffalo. In the second instance five lions had ganged up on the buff. The third time it was three lions.

I've never been able to figure out why the surviving lions didn't eat the dead buffalo. It may be that they were too badly wounded to stick around. I didn't trail their blood spoor very far, but there was plenty of evidence that some of the retreating lions were badly hurt.

In my first year as an apprentice hunter back

about 1911, my hunting boss, Nicobar Jones, was down with fever and I had to hunt alone. My tracker was an old Zulu called Umgugundhlova (the rumbling of an elephant). We were in the Chobe River area of Caprivi's Finger District, a narrow strip of land that juts into Northern Rhodesia along the Angola border. This finger is about 25 miles wide and 175 miles long. I've shot animals in Southwest Africa and had them drop in Angola or in Rhodesia, and vice versa. There have been weird complications over incidents of that kind, but that's another story.

Anyway, it was January. Rains were torrential and making lakes out of lowlands. Lions were on the prowl all night. In those days they used to roar when nights were stormy. It was dusk. Wet and miserable, I followed Umgugundhlova along a wooded ridge, heading back to camp.

Suddenly Umgugundhlova stopped and motioned downhill. A female lion, looking black in the half-light, sneaked along on her belly like a house cat stalking a bird. I raised my rifle, but Umgugundhlova shook his head and pointed ahead. I saw nothing. He put his thumb tips to his ears, pointing his forefingers like horns. He meant buffalo. I searched the murky hillside until I began to see buffalo shapes everywhere. I pointed questioningly to two or three spots, but Umgugundhlova held up one finger—one buffalo.

The lioness squeezed so closely to the ground that her belly must have scraped. She drew her hind legs under her, gathering for a spring. Her tail stuck straight out like a stiff rope. In the same instant another lion roared. A buffalo bellowed in terror. In a flash I saw monstrous action—black silhouettes of violent death dancing grotesquely.

The female lion leaped upon the buffalo's flank, half riding him. A male lion stood on his hind feet and swiped at the buffalo's head. The bellowing buffalo went to his knees but was instantly up, rearing high, his hoofs in the air. His stern swung, his body twisted, and he came down on the male lion with both front feet, stretching the big cat out flat. Then, with the female still clawing and biting at him, he kneeled, and with a sideways motion of his head pushed a horn through his victim's chest.

He had a moment's difficulty getting the horn clear, but when he did, he swung his whole body around in a whipping circle. The lioness was shaken off but leaped again full on his back, where she dug in like a huge tick. I don't know what might have happened next, for I drilled the lioness through the head. At the sound of the shot, the buffalo kicked his heels and took off, to be swallowed almost instantly by the blackness.

The male lion was still alive but dying fast. Umgugundhlova hurried things along with a couple of thrusts of his short spear. He said in Zulu:

"Empty bellies make lion too brave. Male lion scared of buffalo, but female make him help get food."

It's true. Females of all big-game animals have more courage than the males.

J. Fred Russell was an actor. He had come to Africa with some movie outfit and got fired. He didn't want to go home to Hollywood without evidence of his ability as a hunter. He hired me to take him and his cameraman, Schmidt, into game country so he could have his picture taken doing hero stuff.

Russell was as phony as they come. Schmidt looked like a thug.

I shot lions, leopards, rhinos, and kudu, and Schmidt took Russell's picture posing beside each one.

One day Russell pointed a .375 in the direction of a buffalo, shut both eyes, and pulled the trigger. The buff dropped in his tracks. Russell was elated. He told Schmidt to set up the movie camera. Then he improvised a little scenario. He peered from under his palm like the Indian in the *End of the Trail* picture. He sighted along his rifle. He ran toward the dead beast.

The dead buffalo lay flat on one side. Russell took a running jump and landed with both feet on the animal's chest. The buffalo cut loose with a mournful bellow that died away in a sort of sucking wheeze. Russell's weight had squashed the air out of the lungs.

But before the buffalo's bawl had died away, Russell, his rifle thrown aside, was high-tailing it for the brush. He made great bounds like a kangaroo. All the while Schmidt was grinding away.

Schmidt refused to give up that film. He kept it in his tent, hinting that he was going to release it to the world when he got home. Russell managed to get it, and one night he disappeared with two Masai boys. Later I heard he was seen in Nairobi, so I guess he got out of Africa all right.

If you want to make a nice piece of change, get yourself a buffalo head with horns fifty-seven or more inches in spread. There are always a hundred or so phony sportsmen hanging around bars of Nairobi and Johannesburg who will pay you one thousand dollars for record buff horns. Last I heard, the record was fifty-six and one-half inches. Those wealthy bar-fly sportsmen really pay for trophies that prove them mighty hunters.

Two or three years ago those fellows were offering five hundred dollars for a pair of thirty-eight-inch eland horns measured straight, and four hundred dollars for thirty-six roan antelope horns measured on the curve. Fifty-four inch sable antelope horns are worth five hundred dollars, and a pair of sixty-seven-inch kudu horns two thousand dollars.

But record horns are few and far between.

Photo: Carol Resnick

Buffalo in Kenya's Maasai Mara. Don't let their gentle appearance fool you.

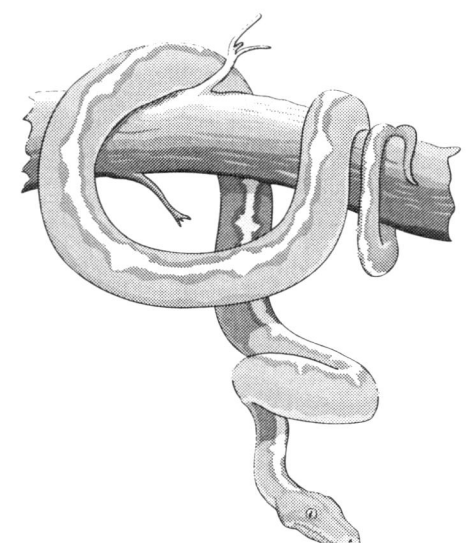

SNAKES

PROBABLY as a defense against subconscious fear, most persons laugh off startling snake stories as fantasy. Yet even the most imaginative liar would have difficulty in concocting tales to equal the astonishing and deadly activities of Africa's pythons, vipers, cobras, mambas, and adders.

If you go a-hunting in Africa, your chances of being bitten by a snake are *three times greater* than those of being killed by a wild animal. One must be remarkably agile to evade the lightning-like, hissing strike of an angry cobra. No man can run fast enough to evade the attack of the sleek twelve-foot black mamba, the "Snake-That-Walks-on-Its-Tail" or, as the Zulus call it, *Muriti-Wa-Lesu* (The Shadow-of-Death). Fortunately, except in mating season or when shut off from his hide-out, this killer, found chiefly in South and Central Africa, seldom attacks humans.

British army records of the Zulu War tell of an officer on horseback who was bitten by a black mamba. The man died within a few minutes.

There's the green mamba, a six-foot, whip-like

tree dweller, green as grass, that hangs from a limb over a trail and drives his fangs into the back of your neck as you pass. I know of no man bitten by this green assassin who lived more than an hour.

In South Africa there is the poison-spitting ringhals, a black cobra with two white bands on his chest. He's fast and vicious, sinking his fangs into flesh with a chewing motion—five progressive bites in one second, a double row of five wounds—and with each bite, squirting venom onto the punctures. He is more dangerous than other cobras because he doesn't always wait for you to get close, but squirts poison at you in thin jets. His aim is accurate, and he can hit a man's eye at six feet. Always wear goggles or sunglasses when tangling with a ringhals. His poison in your eye can blind or kill you.

Most authorities on reptiles classify the green mamba and the black mamba as different members of the same family. I disagree. I've never seen a black mamba less than five feet long, nor a green mamba more than six feet long. It's my belief that the mamba is green until about half grown, then turns to olive-black. At the time of color change he also changes habits, moving out of trees to *kopjes* and plains. However, in the adult black phase he's no slouch in a tree either.

How fast is a black mamba? "Authorities" (God bless 'em) dispute this question at great length. Estimates run from four to thirty-five miles an hour.

The black mamba's top speed is about twenty-five miles an hour. I've never held a stop watch on a mamba, but I've held one on a lizard that did a bit better than twenty miles an hour. One summer afternoon in the Potgietersrust District of the Transvaal I watched a black mamba chase one of those same lizards. The lizard had about a fifty-foot start, but the fleeting little rascal was in the mamba's mouth before he had gone seventy yards.

How hard does a mamba strike? He strikes hard enough to knock a man down. I know of an eighteen-year-old white boy who was knocked flat by a striking black mamba and died within an hour. I know of a fifteen-year-old black boy who was knocked down and died within ten minutes.

How vicious can an angry black mamba get? Oom Paul Kruger, first President of Transvaal Republic, tells that one day when he was leading a patrol against the British a black mamba leaped among his men, bit three fatally, then turned on two dogs that chased it and bit them. They died too. The mamba got away.

In Zululand they tell of a green mamba that killed so many men as they passed beneath the tree where he lurked that a council of war was held to devise a plan for destroying it. Several methods were unsuccessfully tried, and men continued to die from mamba wounds on the neck or face. A woman solved the problem.

She cooked a big pot of mealie mush (corn meal), and while it was piping hot placed the kettle on a pad on her head and walked along the trail. The mamba dunked his head in the hot mush and was instantly *pelele* (finished).

Port Elizabeth has a Snake Park where more than

ten thousand visitors a month watch native attendants, wearing gloves, handle all kinds of venomous snakes—vipers, mambas, boom-slangs, adders, and all the grizzly crew. Occasionally a handler is bitten. Unless immediately injected with a general snake serum, he dies. If injection for a mamba bite is delayed even one minute, the bite is fatal. Vipers' poison is not quite so fast. Life can be saved if injection is delayed a few minutes, provided, however, that the wounds are bled and mouth suction is applied to remove the venom.

The human mouth has saved more persons from death by snakebite than all the serums. And the mouth will continue to save more because millions of natives will probably never hear of snake serum.

Until a general serum effective against poisons of all snakes was developed, the "nerve venom" of mambas required different serum than did the "blood venom" of vipers. Men carried both kinds but were sometimes unable to recognize the type snake that bit them—and used the wrong serum. I know of a West African who carried only serum against cobras and who died from the bite of a rhinoceros viper.

Serums are made by milking snakes of their venom and then administering it to horses in small quantities until the horses become immune. Their blood is then drawn, and the watery portion is the snakebite remedy.

Milking the snakes is a chore. The milker grasps the reptile's neck and holds its body under one arm. With his other hand he holds a large glass bowl close to the snake's nose. The snake strikes. Its venom drips into the bowl—one two-hundred-fiftieth of an ounce. Because snakes are milked only once a month during seven months of the year, it requires many snakes to furnish one pound of poison.

Injection of serum itself is not sufficient to stave off death. Circulation must be shut off between wounds and the heart by means of a tourniquet. Two cuts, to the depth of the fang punctures, must be made at right angles across each of the wounds and the poisoned blood sucked out by mouth or by an effective suction instrument. Each time the mouth is emptied it must be rinsed with a solution of permanganate of potash. When the wound is drained and washed, the tourniquet may be removed.

Almost certainly the patient will show signs of giddiness and weakness. Alcohol is not a snakebite cure but a heart stimulant—in small doses—so the patient may be given small shots of whiskey or brandy from time to time.

Keep the wounds open and draining for fifteen days even if all signs of poison have disappeared.

Until I die I'll probably break into a sweat each time I recall the morning I killed my first mamba. It was in 1909 and I was sixteen. My father had been called to Potgietersrust to see what could be done about controlling an epidemic fever that had broken out among the M'shangaans of the district. I can't recall why he took me along—probably to keep me out of mischief.

One morning a donkey belonging to our party

was bitten by a mamba. The donkey died that night, swollen twice its normal size. I got a yen to kill one of those devil-snakes and borrowed a shotgun from a farmer named Philip Amm.

I knew better than to mention the mamba and inferred that I was going after duikerbok—a pretty little thirty-five-pound antelope. Next morning, four hours and about six miles after I'd started, I got into two-foot-high grass. I began to get nervous. When I saw a flat-topped rock about four feet high not far away, I headed for it, intending to take a breather before starting back.

I was within a few paces of the rock when two mambas reared beside it, one head a foot above the grass, the other almost two feet above. I was so frightened that I've no recollection of shooting—but I did. Both mambas disappeared. Next thing I remember is being on top of the rock, looking down at the smaller of the snakes threshing about. I saw no sign of the other. I shot the wounded mamba again. With a series of little convulsions it turned belly-up. Then its only movement was a twitching tail.

Scared almost witless, I sat on that hot rock for what must have been an hour. I didn't dare get off, for I feared the other mamba would return.

I tried to calm myself by noticing what went on around me. A honey bird circled, screaming. A tock-tock beetle tapped the ground beside the dead snake with his abdomen. The grass, bending under a breeze, turned from bronze to silver, then back to bronze as the breeze sped on its way. Through the heat haze the *kopjes* loomed dark purple at moments and vanished entirely at others. I looked at the sky, head thrown back. Not a cloud.

I looked back to the shimmering belly of the snake, and sweat seemed to squirt from my palms. The other mamba—the male, I guessed, because of its size—was writhing over and around the dead one, pushing at her with his snout.

I shook so hard that the muzzle of the shotgun played a small tattoo on the rock. Quicker than thought, that black mamba whipped into coils and reared his head four feet high. I whimpered and backed to the far edge of the rock. The mamba darted forward and, with only his head above the rock's rim, stared at me.

I fired. The head vanished. For a long time I was afraid to move. I knew he could slither to the top of the rock in less than a second. After a while, with my gun at the ready, I moved across that flat surface, one shaky step at a time. Headless, the male lay across his mate.

I was still afraid to get off the rock. It was midafternoon when I finally decided to take a chance. I moved for a final look at the mambas. Both were gone!

I probably would have starved up there on my stony perch had I not seen five passing Kaffirs and yelled. When they got close enough to understand, I told them about the snakes. They immediately spread out and came forward, shouting and beating the grass with their knobkerries.

Still atop the rock, I asked where the snakes had gone. One of the Kaffirs reached down to the base of the rock and pulled the snakes into view by their tails. He said they'd been dragged by a jackal. Maybe so, but in nightmares I still feel they vanished through sorcery.

One popular misconception about snakes is that the poisonous ones have broad, flat heads and stubby tails. Some have, particularly vipers, but many deadly snakes are slender-bodied, with small heads and tapering tails. There's probably no more graceful snake on earth than the mamba.

Another misconception is that all cobras have hoods that distend when the snake is enraged. That isn't true either. Mambas belong to the cobra family and haven't even the semblance of a hood, although they can swell their necks a little by distending their windpipes.

Cobras are the most vicious and most untamable of all snakes. There are nine kinds of them in Africa: the Egyptian, the yellow, the black-lipped, the black-necked, the yellow-headed, Gold's cobra, Guenther's cobra, and of course the mamba and ringhals.

Many times I've stood with a 12-gauge shotgun not ten feet from ringhals while Cameraman Bob Schlick photographed the spitting demons through a pane of glass fastened to the front of the camera.

Schlick would leer happily through wide goggles as each ringhals reared upward, hood flaring, lower jaw drawn back so its fangs hung cleared for action. Schlick would wave. The snake would tip its head back, point its fang tips toward the camera, and let go with two thin jets of venom. Sometimes they'd spray the glass shield of the camera, sometimes Schlick's goggles, sometimes both.

They seemed so evil, so utterly fiendish, that I was hard put to it to keep from blowing them to pieces. In fact, once in a while I did so, much to Schlick's annoyance.

My encounters with black-necked cobras have been numerous. I've known several natives to be killed by them, but few white men. A cobra's short fangs are unable to penetrate clothing of reasonable thickness. Nevertheless, he's a dangerous customer. He will sometimes attack without provocation. He's greased lightning and will coil, rear, strike, and recoil in less than a second. All cobras bite like bulldogs, hang on, and *start chewing*.

Their lower jaws are two practically straight bones joined at the ends by a ligament like an elastic rubber band. Either side of the jaw can be moved independently, and chewing is accomplished by sort of walking their recurved teeth through flesh. With each chew, poison is squirted. After four or five seconds, when they let go, their job has been well done.

I don't believe that any other creature has so vile a disposition as the cobra. While the king cobra of India gets most of the publicity because of fantastic markings on his hood, the less colorful cobras of Africa are every whit as vicious.

One day as I walked through a forest in Uganda a cobra was chewing on my right trouser leg above the ankle before I knew he existed. I kicked out violently. He held on. I swung my leg about. He still held on, his body flailing like a whip. I finally managed to hold him by stepping on his tail. I jerked my pants leg from his teeth. The snake darted into the brush.

A minute later he was after me again. He reared beside the trail, his hood wide, and hissed like a leaky steam pipe. Knowing my clothing was sufficient protection, I stepped toward him. He struck and missed, but the force of his thrust made him skid forward on his belly at least a foot. Instantly he recoiled, reared, and struck again. I pulled my leg out of range. Again he missed and slid toward me. We repeated the maneuver until he had jerked himself all the way across the trail.

I moved off a few paces, and the cobra darted after me. When close, he stopped and, rearing high, hissed with hatred. I knocked him galleywest with the barrel of my rifle.

Those hardy souls who travel through Africa in shorts and bare knees are asking for it. Sometimes they get it. There are more poisonous snakes in Africa than is generally believed. Old hunters think Africa's snake population at least ten times greater than popular estimate.

This refusal to admit that there are far more snakes than are seen is common to all nationalities. Many Englishmen are shocked when told that the deadly common viper inhabits their fair island. Irishmen deny with heat, and sometimes with profanity, that vipers are frequently killed in supposedly snakeless Eire.

Late in World War II, I went deer hunting in Southern California. Every member of the party was an old-time sportsman who, with rifle and fishing rod, had ranged throughout the West. Over fried potatoes and broiled rabbit one evening the talk turned to rattlesnakes. Said one grizzled Nimrod:

"There're three species of rattlesnakes in America."

"Five," someone contradicted.

The argument went back and forth without agreement. Someone turned to me and said:

"There's the diamondback, the sidewinder, mountain, timber, and red rattlers. Do you know of any others?"

"Well, I've been studying up on rattlers," I said, "and the books say that America has twenty-six species and at least thirteen are at home right here in California."

I got a horselaugh. When it comes to snakes, most people won't believe.

But the books are right. There are twenty-six species of rattlesnakes in North America.

African cobras lay eggs, about twenty at a time, and newly hatched youngsters are fully capable of taking care of themselves. They immediately proceed to do so by disappearing. They know they're small, hence easy prey to enemies, including cannibal snakes. They're seldom seen by man until fully grown. All vipers except the Cape viper, bear their young alive, usually twelve to fifteen at a time. These deadly little rascals disappear like the young cobras.

Few snakes, except during breeding season, show themselves to man if they can sneak away.

I'm sure that for every snake a man sees he's walked within yards of a dozen.

In southern Ethiopia I once followed a wounded leopard into a dry, almost bare, rocky ravine which came to a dead end within seventy-five yards of the entrance. No leopard. As I entered I saw a snake wriggle into a crevice on the ravine side. Walking out, I saw another disappear behind a rock. That was all. Two snakes.

Next morning when I returned to the ravine I found that natives had built a fire at the far end. Draft from the hills was pushing the feeble blaze toward the ravine mouth. The blaze jumped with sudden spurts from one meager grass tuft to another. Here and there flames stopped to dally with bits of dried wood and leaves. The fire moved slowly, with little smoke. Ahead of it wriggled big snakes, little snakes, harmless snakes, and venomous snakes. Some slithered down ravine sides; some leaped. Lizards raced for safety. Beetles and bugs churned their legs frantically. The snakes flowed over them.

Across the mouth of the ravine the natives had dug a ditch about three feet deep and two feet wide. Into this the snakes fell and flopped until it held at least two hundred. The fire died, but smoke continued to drift along the ground. The snakes writhed. Some tangled into balls. Strangely, none made an attempt to get out.

The natives, mostly Kaffirs, filled in the ditch, burying the snakes alive. They explained that a man had been bitten in that ravine two or three days before and that this was revenge.

The point here is that there were actually two hundred snakes in the area where I had seen but two.

A man may admire the grace and courage of the cobra, but few fail to shudder at the sight of a big-headed, thick-bodied, short-tailed viper. In my opinion, although some are beautifully colored, vipers are the ugliest creatures on earth. Unlike the cobra, who bites and chews in an effort to do as much damage as possible with his short fangs, the viper opens his mouth wide—about four inches. His long fangs unfold and point outward. He drives them deep into flesh, through pants leg and underwear. Fangs embedded, he bites down, compressing his poison sacs, squirting his venom into the wounds through hollow teeth.

I've encountered only four of the vipers: the three-foot, slender, egg-laying, frog-eating Cape viper; the four-foot rhinoceros viper with unbelievably beautiful markings and colorings; the Gaboon viper with its loathsome head; and the loud-hissing, buff-and-black, four-foot puff adder found almost everywhere in Africa.

To me the startling thing about vipers is that, although dull and sluggish in their movements, they strike with the speed of a light ray.

My experiences with the side-winding Gaboon viper were in Hereroland in Southwest Africa. The first I ever saw was curled in the sand with only his whitish, catlike, upward-protruding eyes above ground level. He tried to outstare me. I stared back. He became uneasy and squirmed away with grotesque sideways loopings, his body edging off at a diagonal from the direction in which his head was pointing.

The Gaboon viper is a subdued study in buff, brown, and purple. Under his eyes are two dark stripes. His nasty, flat, dirty-tan head is an almost circular monstrosity; a great evil, coldly grinning lump which seems far too heavy to be supported by his skinny neck. I once measured a thirty-inch specimen with a belly circumference of six and one half inches, a three-inch tail, and the rest of him, except his head, just bloated body.

Most snakes feel smooth. Not so the rhinoceros viper of West Central Africa. His scales end in small spikes. One wrapped himself around my forearm once, and his spikes lacerated my flesh almost as painfully as a giraffe's tongue once did.

The rhinoceros viper has two horns on his nose. He's the pet of reptile students because of his stunning colors. Nobody could describe him and do him justice. Brilliant blotches of blue, orange, yellow, dark red, and black! His head is blue. A black arrow on the forehead points to the yellow horns. In temperament and habits he's like other vipers.

Puff adders remind me of rattlesnakes. You run across them everywhere in tropical Africa. Because they are the most numerous of the venomous snakes, they've taken the greatest death toll among humans.

The Cape viper is found mostly in the southern tip of Africa and is the embodiment of all misconceptions about harmless snakes: slender body, narrow head, tapering tail. Innocuous as he appears, he is a deadly rascal.

The largest, most fascinating serpent in Africa is the rock python, eighteen feet long. He's a strange fellow, meaner than a frustrated hornet at times, but docile as a rabbit at others. He sometimes kills men but never swallows them. Too big. He has occasionally, according to natives, made a meal of a child, but his usual fare is small antelope, hares, young wild pigs, and any rodent or fowl he can catch.

Like all constrictors, he kills by squeezing. He can crush a thirty-five-pound pig so effectively that he has little trouble getting it down his elastic gullet. He swallows victims headfirst, drawing them into his mouth with curved teeth, then goes through a series of gulps and contortions of jaws, neck, and upper body. Sometimes when his victim is a bit too large for comfortable swallowing the python's eyes pop and the sides of his neck bulge like a cobra's hood. He stops occasionally to breathe through a tube that he forces between his lower jaw and the animal in his mouth. When the victim finally rests in his stomach, the python gapes like a man abruptly wakened from sleep, pulls his dislocated jaws back into place, and wants no more food for two weeks.

Long, long ago pythons walked on legs. They still have them, two horny bumps about where hind legs ought to be. They use them, too, particularly when climbing. Like all snakes, pythons have no ears, but hear with their tongues. They not only hear, but detect sound vibrations inaudible to humans.

Pythons lay eggs, making a nest by curling their bodies around the eggs, and maintain a hatching temperature of seventy-five degrees. Some hunters claim to have seen clutches of between ninety and one hundred eggs. I've never seen more than sixty; usually twenty-five or thirty.

In a dreary, rocky valley in Northern Rhodesia one afternoon in 1922 I sat on the ground almost helpless with a twisted ankle while Ubusuku, my Zulu tracker, engaged in a death battle with the largest python I've ever seen.

I had fallen off a high rock while aiming at a wild hog. The ankle was so painful that I could hardly speak. Ubusuku, wishing to get me under cover for the night, explored a high bank nearby and located a cave. He carried me to the entrance, put me down, and walked inside. Almost immediately he cartwheeled past me, wrapped in a python's embrace.

The python had one loop around the Zulu, pinning down one arm. Ubusuku had the fingers of his free hand around the python's thick neck. In some manner Ubusuku's assagai had gotten pinned between the coil of the snake and his back, the blade up above his head like an Indian feather.

My rifle was useless in so violent an affray. My revolver was even more useless, for I never could shoot one accurately. If the Zulu hadn't been as strong as a bull buffalo, he'd have been quickly crushed. As it was, the python kept banging his snout against Ubusuku's face, but the straining muscles of the black's right arm kept the blows from being effective.

Scattered about were dwarf thornbushes. The python kept whipping his tail, seeking a purchase.

I knew that, once that tail got hold, Ubusuku was done for. Over and over the pair somersaulted. I unsheathed my knife and hunched as close as I could, but they shifted ground too fast for me.

The snake's tail wrapped around a bush. Instantly the python squeezed. I heard Ubusuku groan. I literally threw myself at the bush and with a slashing sweep of my knife severed the tail. The python released Ubusuku, whirled, and banged his snout against the bleeding tail stump. Ubusuku staggered, picked up his assagai, and, as the python moved toward him again, drove the blade through its neck. Then the Zulu threw himself clear and stood grinning as the big snake, assagai dangling, threshed about blindly before dying with weird hissing noises.

That python weighed at least two hundred pounds—about the same as Ubusuku.

It was Ubusuku who taught me that if a snake has a choice of two objects to strike at he'll choose the warmer one. He also warned me never to go without protection for my legs from snakes. Yet Ubusuku always went naked except for shorts. He wouldn't even wear shoes.

Corel Professional Photos CD-ROM

The Hippopotamus, the prized "River Horse" of the Ancient Egyptians.

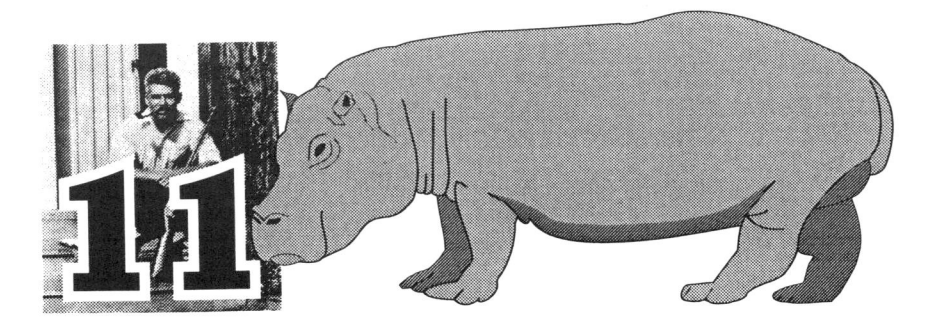

HIPPOS

ACTING AS GUIDE for sportsmen-hunters is often a vexatious job. Even in a party of two, jealousies and resentments erupt when luck of the hunt favors one more than the other. Parties of three almost invariably develop feuds when one man consistently bags the most or the largest trophies. In parties of four or five, particularly if weather is uncomfortable, bickerings, accusations, and heated arguments usually become the order of the day. No old-time white hunter will take out more than two if he can help it. He prefers to take only one.

The cause of most unpleasantness is the inability of sportsmen to decide which way they want the rule of "first blood." Does the animal belong to the man who first wounded it or to the man who killed it? I always tried to settle that question before starting out, but unhappily sportsmen often forget agreements once they've blooded game.

The first signs of discontent are usually complaints about spiders in blankets, ants in the jam, and other minor annoyances. Trouble builds up from there.

Nationality of sportsmen doesn't make much difference. Americans "blow their tops" with most noise. Englishmen get sullen. Frenchmen and Italians pout. Norwegians get stubborn. Portuguese quit. Germans mumble to themselves. Prussians get haughty.

The guide goes about his business as best he can, hoping his next party will consist of men who have achieved maturity. He speaks only enough to maintain authority, swallowing his personal vexations, trip after trip, until a time comes when he can close shop and go on a binge in Luanda, Bulawayo, Mombasa, or anywhere he can work up an alcoholic fog to obliterate memories of tourist hunters. Or he may go home and raise a crop of vegetables.

My refreshment, when I could no longer stand being nursemaid, used to be a solitary hippo hunt.

There's nothing sporting about shooting hippos. They're plentiful in many African rivers and are easily killed with even a small-caliber bullet in the brain. They require no spooring, no belly-crawling stalking. When wounded on land they take to the water and you get an easy second shot.

The rhino, with his idiotic antics, gives men hearty laughs. The hippo gives them quiet chuckles. His monstrous mouth, dinky tail, small, eager ears; his astonishing facial expressions, weird grunts, bellows, burps, blowings, and suckings, all tickle a man's risibilities.

When a hippo plays you a dirty trick, you can't stay angry at him for long. His most violent moods are funny. Despite numerous tales of his stentor-voiced rampages, he's really no more dangerous than a domestic Berkshire boar. Almost everybody loves the hippo.

Then why kill him?

Well, there's money in him for the hunter. A head with canine tusks of thirty inches or more brings a good price. One with two fifty-inch tusks brings a small fortune, maybe one thousand dollars. A head with even one unusually long tusk is well worth bagging.

Hippos' canine and incisor teeth never stop growing. Normally they're kept worn down by the grinding of uppers against lowers. However, when an upper canine tooth breaks off, the lower one has nothing to prevent growth, and grow it does. I believe the record tooth is sixty-four inches measured on the curve.

Hippo teeth are unusually hard and in early days were much used to make false human teeth. Many a sportsman in those days went hunting hippo while wearing teeth from one of the beast's ancestors in his own plates.

If a hippo has an uncomfortably long canine or incisor tooth, he's usually mean, but if you know hippos, even the meanest aren't too dangerous. Say he attacks your boat, tipping it over and dunking you. Take a deep breath and swim ashore under water. The old curmudgeon will be snorting around on the surface near the boat, waiting for you to come up. However, there's small chance of a hippo actually attacking. Most boats capsized by hippos just happened to be over a spot where one of the brutes surfaced. Naturally, when a three- or four-ton river horse bangs his back against the keel, you're going a-swimmin'. That happened to me once, and I didn't wait to view the hippo's facial expression. I practically scampered across the bottom of the river on hands and knees.

I stood once on a riverbank and saw the canoe of two friends upset by a rising hippo. Strange how calm and deliberate a man can be when a witness instead of an actor in a perilous episode. Ignoring the humans, I watched the hippo. He treaded water for a moment, ears wigwagging like mad. The upturned canoe swung toward him. He sucked in air and went down like a sounding whale. He emerged a couple of minutes later in the center of a raft of lily pads with only his head showing. He bugged his eyes and wriggled his ears in obvious panic. My friends waded ashore and wanted to shoot him, but their rifles were at the bottom of the river. I wouldn't lend them mine, figuring that the hippo's fright was sufficient punishment for his carelessness.

I've heard and read many tales of hippos charging boats and crushing them in their jaws. This does happen. Whenever possible, I've checked such stories. In every case I've found two conditions present: (a) baby hippos were about, and (b) crocodiles were numerous.

Now a hippo doesn't know what a boat is. All he knows is that it looks like a croc and seems to be threatening the youngsters. His rage is terrible, for crocs and hippos have a sort of treaty that permits crocs to live among hippos *except when babies are young*. When a crocodile violates the agreement, no diplomatic notes are exchanged, no truce talks held. The hippo nearest the invader, male or female, promptly bites him in half.

The serious-minded, inoffensive hippo is not normally a killer. He has no false pride and will usually retreat rather than fight. Yet he will not flee from a crocodile.

The young of all animals are delightful. Lion and leopard cubs are sweet-tempered little shavers. Buffalo and wildebeest calves are gentle and trusting. Zebra colts and the young of giraffe are beautiful. An elephant toto is a lovable little clown. But my favorites are the big-headed, stub-tailed, fat little hippo piglets. Women invariably call them adorable.

In the water, chiefly as protection from crocodiles, the whitish hippo babies ride on their mothers' necks. As they grow older they move to her back. On land the little rascals usually waddle a few feet, then flop on their stomachs, place their heads on their forelegs, and go to sleep. One would think them ordinary little pigs.

Hippos are great eaters and sleepers. They feed mainly on grasses and herbage on riverbanks, often going a half mile inland in search of a snack. Usually they travel well-worn, deep-rutted trails, the ruts running side by side like those of a narrow-chassis truck. Often there's a third, smaller rut between the ones made by the hippos' feet. That's where they've dragged their over-stuffed bellies.

In dry season hippos always find their way back to the river even when they've wandered off their usual trails. They sniff the air, locate direction of the water, and amble home. During heavy rains, however, when river scent is drowned in the downpour, the big beasts get lost. This sometimes makes them panicky, and they put their heads down and barge every which way through the underbrush. If a man can't get out of their way, he'll be run over by them. To be stepped on by a three- or four-ton hippo is an undignified way to die.

Hippos also feed on young reeds, grasses, and weeds that sometimes grow on river bottoms, but they'll always leave water to feed on land when vegetation is luxuriant. They eat mostly at night.

I've never seen a man killed by a hippo, but I've seen several scared nearly to death. One was a small, spindle-legged Scotsman with a large head. His name was Peter Stephens. He was from Aberdeen, and he went right back there after meeting with the hippo.

We were hunting young hippos and smoking the hams for a wealthy gourmet named L. Sam Marx. Stephens had come along to build the smokehouse and to see that the hams were cured according to Marx's exacting demands. Marx was one of those strange epicures who have yens for unusual, outlandish foods. The chef at the Union Club in Johannesburg, where Marx frequently ate, once told me that among dishes prepared especially for Marx on one occasion were:

Python fillets broiled in browned butter.

Baby porcupine and kidney pie.

Iced Portuguese oysters shipped from France.

Ostrich egg scrambled with Gorgonzola cheese, sour cream, chives, and burnet.

Hippopotamus ham steam-fried in sherry and brown sugar.

There are hundreds of rich gourmets like Marx throughout Europe. Some go to Africa for the sole purpose of enjoying certain game dishes. They take all necessary spices and ingredients and usually do their own cooking. They're an unusual lot, and often so finicky about meats that many will eat no antelope except the klipspringer. Others, apparently with less sensitive tastes, will eat eland and bushbuck. All, however, scorn the meat of all other antelope. Some delight in a monitor lizard aspic served with broiled fish.

Stephens wasn't a chef. He had achieved fame for cured ham specialties. Marx would eat no hippo except that from heavily foliaged sections of western African rivers. He said hippo meat from dry areas had no savor.

Marx ranked hippo hams, young American tom turkey, shrimps *alla fra diavolo,* and Iowa apple pie among the most delectable viands on earth. He had been having hippo hams cured for years, sending many as gifts to the world's great. Among recipients, I was told, were Theodore Roosevelt and King Leopold II of Belgium.

This particular hippo hunt was back in 1912— one of the first jobs I undertook on my own. It was also Stephens' first trip to Africa. My instructions from Marx were to go to the Zambezi about seventy-five miles west of Victoria Falls and to bag five hippos whose hams would weigh not less than eighty nor more than one hundred twenty pounds. This meant hippos weighing not more than three thousand pounds on the hoof.

Late in April, Stephens and I, with three Hottentots and two unusually tall Bushmen, arrived at a beautiful spot on the banks of a tributary of the Zambezi. Reeds along the banks were of heavy growth but had not yet fallen in annoying crisscross fashion, which makes walking through them almost impossible.

Rains had been spasmodic but plentiful. Marshes and lowlands still held lots of water. Vegetation was varied, heavy and tender-green. Hippo tunnels through the reeds were everywhere. Otters' trails were numerous, for shallow waters were full of fish. Saw-toothed grass fringed edges of the sloughs, making the going tough on the bare-legged natives.

Nights were filled with hippo noises: splashings, weird whistlings, and coughings. Each morning found Stephens more nervous. He got so he wouldn't step into water if he could help it, but stood back a little, his big head wagging from side to side. Nor would he walk in grass more than a foot high.

In the wagon he had brought hogsheads, nitrates, salt, sugar, and a large chest packed with spices and herbs—horehound, pennyroyal, lavender, germander, hyssop, cloves, and wild marjoram. He had also brought bags of willow sawdust to flavor the smoke. The Bushmen were to build a smokehouse from woven reeds and branches, but near the little eminence where we made camp Stephens spotted a hollow baobab tree and decided it might make a satisfactory smokehouse instead.

The tree was big—probably sixty-five feet in diameter at the base. The hollow, large enough to hold two hippos side by side, extended far up in the trunk. Stephens' head wagging like a pendulum, stared for so long at the tree that I asked: "What's the matter?"

"I'd like to build a fir-re inside. Do you think the tr-ree wud bur-rn doon?"

"You couldn't burn a baobab tree with a gasoline fire," I told him, and almost regretted I had spoken, for his head began wagging harder than ever. He piled dried grass inside, lighted it, and stood back, staring upward. The grass burned without smoke, so Stephens threw green branches on. Within a few minutes smoke began curling from vents far above ground.

"A guid dr-raft," Stephens said. "Th' Lor-rd is wuth me."

He was a happy little man as he set out barrels and began measuring ingredients for brine. He hummed through his nose, whistled through his teeth, and talked to hirnself.

After I again assured him that the tree would not burn, he built a roaring fire inside and sprinkled spices on the flames, "to give a bonny-smellin' char," he explained.

A few days later at dusk I returned to camp feeling pretty good myself. I had bagged a fat yearling hippo. The boys had skinned it and were not far behind me, carrying four fat hams. The Kaffirs were happy, too, for they would soon be enjoying an orgy of their favorite meat.

I yelled for Stephens but got no answer. I yelled for his two Bushmen helpers. No response. I lifted the covers off four hogsheads and waited for my boys. I wondered vaguely about Stephens, for I knew he was too leery of animals to leave camp even with his helpers.

After the hams had been dropped in the brine and the barrels covered, I walked toward the "smokehouse" tree. Within a foot of the tent-shaped opening were two hippo tracks. Sign showed that the hippo had backed a few yards, turned at right angles, and trotted toward the slough. Puzzled, I went back to the tree entrance and looked inside.

There lay Stephens—out like a fallen candle.

After I dragged him into the open and revived him, he sat up, looked around in bewilderment, then in tones of horror said: "Na, na, na, na, na!" covering his face with his hands and throwing himself backward on the ground.

For an hour all I could learn was that he wanted to leave for Livingstone at once. He kept saying:

"I canna stand it. I willna stand it."

Finally I got the story. He had been inside the tree putting up crosspieces from which to hang meat hooks. The Bushmen had been puttering about outside. After a time he called to them, and when they didn't answer he went out to find them. They weren't in sight. Stephens wasn't surprised, because the two were always going off on jaunts of their own. He went back to the coolness inside the tree, grew drowsy, and napped.

He was awakened by a series of grunts, got to his hands and knees, and timidly put his head through the entrance just as a hippo began to peek inside.

Half hysterically Stephens described it:

"His filthy gr-reat face touched mine. That awful, slaverrin' mug. Then he groaned like. I r-remember-r no mor-re."

I wanted to laugh, but the man was suffering shock. He would lie quietly a few minutes, then moan:

"Gr-reat God! Gr-reat God!"

After thinking the episode over, I decided that the hippo had become fascinated by the odors of spices and had failed to scent man-smell because of them.

Anyway, in the morning Stephens still insisted on going to Livingstone, so about noon, after showing me how to mix formulas for brine and maintain the smoldering fires, he left with one of the Hottentots.

After the boy returned to camp he said Stephens had advised him to "go and live in Scotland wherre ther-re ar-re no such gr-ruesome goings-on."

I guess I did all right with the hams, for when I delivered them in July, Marx made no complaint. But I've not heard of Stephens since.

During most of the year male hippos pal around together in harmony, browsing at the same bushes and using one another for pillows during afternoon siestas. But in breeding season they stage uproarious battles for leadership of the herd. The hide of almost every adult male hippo I've seen bears scars from such fights.

A deposed leader loses all interest in females and leads a solitary life. Occasionally he becomes an embittered outlaw and attacks almost anything. He delights in crashing out from behind bushes when natives pass, frightening the poor devils into hysteria. It's from such terrified Kaffirs that most of the fantastic hippo tales come. A Kasai once told me he had been chased by a hippo "with two mouths."

Ordinarily a rogue hippo will bite whatever part of your body is handiest. In water, however, he almost always goes after the legs; probably because they're kicking. To escape a charging hippo on land, all one has to do is to get behind a fallen log or some other low barrier. Hippos seldom step over anything that might scrape their bellies.

The ostrich lays his long neck on the ground when hiding from danger. That's smart. The hippo hides his body among foliage and then sticks his head out into the open. That's dumb. He looks so much like one of those ball-dodging characters at fairs that its difficult to keep from throwing stones. Once when I saw one of the behemoths smirking at me from a bush, I did just that. As the stone bounced off the beast's grotesque mug, an expression of horror crossed his face and, burping violently from both ends, he hurled himself from a high riverbank into the water.

Mean hippo rogues, however, are few and far between. Most of the poor Ishmaels accept their fate philosophically. Some spend hours each day sitting on their backsides watching their former companions sporting in the pools. When herds come ashore, the old rogues lumber away, sometimes wandering far off to see the world.

The most famous of touring hippos was Hubert, a three-tonner who in the early 1940s shook the mud of his native Swaziland swamp from his feet and set out to see the wonders of South Africa. For more than thirty months Hubert upset theories of zoologists and scientists by hiking at a steady mile-a-day gait along highways and byways of the Transvaal and Natal. He plodded more than one thousand miles, visiting kraals, villages, farms, and cities. His progress was recorded daily in most African and European newspapers.

Because rain frequently came soon after Hubert passed through a district, Kaffirs began worshiping him as a rain god. Even some whites did too. His progress became a triumphal tour, farmers and villagers welcoming the great river horse with piles of tasty cabbages, celery, and sugar cane. When such fare was not provided, Hubert entered fields and, using his great teeth, plowed up his own dinner.

He enjoyed people but showed only mild interest in automobiles. He seemed to be of a religious turn of mind, for he lingered longer in churchyards than anywhere else. He made himself at home at a Bhuddist monastery for three days and left only after he had eaten most of its garden shrubs and flowers. He spent a day now and then at Hindu temples.

Near Johannesburg, about two hundred miles from Swaziland, Hubert turned sharply southeast and headed for Durban three hundred miles away.

On and on he plodded, stopping for a few days in a swamp known as Honeymoon Creek. Romanticists insist that Hubert stopped to enjoy a love affair, but zoologists think he stopped merely to cool his bunions.

Durban planned a civic celebration on Hubert's arrival, but Hubert paused at the city limits to partake of a great bundle of sugar cane donated by the city fathers. All might have gone well had it not been for a sign atop the forage that read: "Welcome, Hubert."

This seemed to upset the guest of honor, and despite the fact that he had been declared a "ward of Natal Province" and accorded protection of the police, Hubert evaded public acclaim by making a detour and entering the city by way of Victoria Park. There he dined on exotic tropical flowers before strolling up West Street. He helped himself to guavas and loquats from fruit stands he passed and stood a long time before a movie theater, gazing at a poster of Judy Garland.

While munching a cabbage, Hubert lifted his big snout and sniffed. Water! Dribbling bits of leaf, he hurried to the city water reservoir and had himself a bath. He was lured away with carrots, celery, and hay. Refreshed, and weary at last of people who tried to scratch his back, rickshas and honking cars, he headed out of town en route for East London, more than 250 miles down the coast. He had done about 225 of those miles and was standing one afternoon in the center of a road, contemplating some bright red blossoms, when a blackguardly white man shot and killed him. Natives insist that Hubert's murderer was a certain Boer farmer. But police could never hang it on him.

In 1953 a full-size statue of Hubert will be erected in Victoria Park by the citizens of Durban.

Hippos are mysterious. They do things that defy explanation. For instance, they sprawl all over each other when taking afternoon naps. A herd of ten average-size adult hippos weighs twenty tons. Yet down in the bottom of that pile of snoozing hippos are the babies, resting securely and comfortably. They always emerge unsquashed.

Another mystery is how a three-ton hippo, four and one-half feet high at the shoulder, can disappear in a pool only two feet deep. It's impossible, of course, yet they do it all the time. Somehow, they flatten out. Even Marius Maxwell, probably the greatest camera hunter of all time, has no explanation.

The sex of a hippo, it seems to me, should be of interest only to another hippo. But to an excitable Mexican zoologist named Angel Galinda, it was extremely important. Galinda was a neat little man with a fair complexion and straight black hair. He spoke no English. I spoke no Spanish. He had appealed to Portuguese government officials at Luanda for a white hunter who would help him get hippo specimens. They put him on to me. My understanding was that he wanted to delve into the animals' internal organs.

Like all zoologists and taxidermists I've taken into hunting country, Galinda was equipped with an assortment of beautiful knives, scissors, scalpels, saws, needles, tubes, and gadgets. I hired twenty Bailundes as carriers and camp boys, and on July 4, 1912, we took off for the Cubango River about two hundred miles east of Benguela. We camped at a point where the Cubango was deep and narrow. Aquatic plants growing on the river bottom covered the surface of the stream with great leaves and flowers. Hippos swarmed in quiet currents.

One or two of our Bailundes understood Portuguese and spoke a little English. They understood Galinda's sputtering Spanish. When Galinda got his dissecting tent set up and his instruments glittering on a white oilcloth-covered table, he signified that he was ready for a hippo. He put his arm around my waist and repeated what sounded like "lembra." I nodded, thinking he meant "hippo," and ambled off to the riverbank. I caught a male hippo nicely behind the ear with a .303, and the natives dragged him to camp.

Galinda looked pleased for a second, then rushed over to the dead beast, looked at its belly, and began dancing and swearing. He tore at his hair, pulled his ears, patted himself below the belt, and behaved like a man stung *by* a tarantula.

Finally he rushed to his tent. I asked Bahita, the head boy, what Galinda was so worked up about. The boy said:

"Him want mama. You shoot papa."

I said: "For gosh sakes!" and went to Galinda's tent. He wouldn't speak.

That night our twenty natives tucked away at least one hundred pounds of good red meat. They'd eat until their bellies ached, lie groaning until the spasms stopped, then begin eating again. They did this over and over, finally sleeping like dead men, only to get up at dawn and start tucking it in again.

I shot a female hippo that afternoon, and Galinda flung himself at her with razor-edged knives. He worked like mad for two days, slashing at the hippo's insides and making notes in a small brown book. At dusk that second day he screeched something in Spanish and began kissing his hand to the treetops.

Next morning, with a nasty, whitish specimen of something or other in a half-gallon glass jar, little Galinda took off for Benguela with five of the Kaffirs, leaving me with the rest of them to break camp and get the stuff back to the coast.

At Benguela I learned he had left by boat for South America, still excited, still hugging his jar.

Since man first walked the earth he has been fascinated by hippos. They were one of the main attractions in China's Intelligence Park, the world's first zoo, established by Emperor Chou about 1100 B.C. For thousands of years the hippo has been sacred to Egyptians of Papremis Island. Ancient Jews called him the behemoth.

The hippo is the most easily captured of all large African animals. Bring-'em-back-alive hunters sometimes spend vast sums to take the big brutes. Two teen-age kids could do it as well with an expenditure of a few dollars for rope, canvas, and a couple of shovels.

Orders for live hippos are usually for yearlings, and contracts call for several months' feeding in animal depots before shipment to Europe. This is to condition the captives to foods they'll be eating as inmates of zoos.

The capture of hippos by lone white hunters is done chiefly by their natives. Occasionally Ubusuku, my big Zulu tracker, would make a capture singlehanded. He'd dig a three-foot-deep, cone-shaped pit on a hippo trail, cover it with branches and reeds, and wait for a hippo to drop into it. The sloping sides of the hole forced the hippo's feet together, holding him helpless. Ubusuku would then noose the animal's snout, bandage its eyes, slip a long rope around the belly, then dig dirt away from a side of the pit until he could cinch up the four feet. The belly rope was worked back until stopped by the hind legs, then tightened until the hippo groaned with pressure. Kaffirs hauled him from the pit into a canvas which was wrapped around him until only his nose showed. The belly rope was then loosened, and Mr. Hippo was on his way.

Natives often spear hippos with a harpoon fastened to one end of a rope and a heavy rock fastened at the other end. After a long, agonizing struggle sometimes lasting for hours, the hippo dies. I've even known some white men to use this method, but never an American, nor a Britisher.

Early African explorers like Livingstone, Stanley, Speke, Du Chaillu, Burton, Grant, and Baker wrote of the hippo as a roaring, cruel killer. He certainly scared those fellows. Not only did they misjudge his nature, but they swallowed all tales of hippo atrocities told by natives. Worse, they passed those tales along.

Few contacts with the hippo are dangerous. However, try to avoid meeting one in a hippo tunnel. Along many African rivers, particularly west of Victoria Falls, reeds grow tall and thick. When the reeds stand erect, it's difficult to push through them, but when bent and falling in all directions, they're a tangle that can be forced only with axes or heavy knives. I've seen the going so tough that a whole day was required to make a quarter of a mile.

Hippos push tunnels through such reed-woven jungles. The tunnels permit them to travel to and fro but are seldom large enough for the beasts to turn around in. Consequently, once the animals start, they must go on until they reach the other end. No man with good sense will make use of such tunnels unless certain that no hippos are near. Yet men do it. I did it—once.

And I met a hippo.

In the summer of 1922 I had been guiding a Portuguese surveying party in southeastern Angola. It had been strenuous work, and when an opportunity came to take a couple of weeks off I decided to do a little quiet hunting. I had long had an order for red lechwe horns thirty-five inches or more long. I decided to try for them.

I took three Ovampo boys down to the swampy lechwe country along the Chobe River. We scouted several herds for satisfactory horns, most of the time in water up to our knees. I finally wounded a big buck with horns that looked to be what I wanted. We followed him into high grass and reeds where there was no breeze and heat was like an oven.

An hour of slogging brought us to the lechwe, dead, his head in the water. The horns were two inches short. Disgusted, I sent him back to camp with the Kaffirs and, hoping to find a cool place along the river to enjoy a night's rest, I began forcing a passage. The farther I pushed, the tougher the going. Papyrus palms began mingling with the reeds. Climbing vines bound both together into an almost impenetrable mass.

Clothes steaming, bones and muscles aching, I threw myself again and again at barriers, finally crashing through into a hippo tunnel. Cool air flowed along it, and I sat gulping it in. Still sitting, I dried out the rifle barrel and wiped off the cartridges. Then, without a thought of hippo, I went stooping and sloshing down the tunnel.

Suddenly I heard a hippo snort behind me. Evidently my noises had panicked him and he was now rushing for the river. Nothing stops a frightened hippo when heading for the safety of water. I began a stumbling, stooping run. My rifle snagged. I dropped it. I tripped and sprawled on my belly. The rest of my flight was on hands and feet like a baboon. I skidded and scrambled, the hippo on my tail.

Clear of the tunnel, I jumped to one side just as that mountain of hippo plunged past. He belly-flopped into the Chobe.

I'd been scared in the tunnel, but now I had the jim-jams. It took me a while to realize I wasn't squashed flat. It took me longer to get nerve enough to go back in and get my rifle.

I had been a fool and almost paid for it. Then came a thought that cheered me a bit—the hippo had been just as frightened as I.

12

ANTELOPE

THERE IS SATISFACTION in African antelope hunting beyond anything the big-game hunter will ever know. There can be violence, too, for wounded kudu, sable, or bushbuck can be ugly customers whose slashing hoofs and sweeping horns can kill as surely as lions' fangs and claws.

None but hardy old professionals ever hunt big game by themselves. Others employ trackers and native hunters to bring the animals to bay, leaving the hunter to do the shooting only. Today in many parts of Africa, "tourist" safaris have made a mockery of the word "hunting" so far as big game is concerned.

Not so with antelope. With antelope, a man can, if he wishes, pit his brains, stamina, courage, and hunting craft against the animal's wariness, instincts, and acute senses. A man can do his own spooring and stalking, the most fascinating parts of any hunt. He can do without the aid of natives, for despite assertions to the contrary, any man with normal health and intelligence can become a capable African antelope hunter in sixty days even if he's never before shot a rifle or hunted so much as a rabbit.

He'll have to have a teacher, of course, preferably an old-type white hunter. And he'll have to work at it, for two months isn't much time in which to absorb a lot of animal lore and develop satisfactory marksmanship with a rifle.

The most apt neophyte to whom I ever taught the mysteries of hunting was a thirty-five-year-old German-Swiss geologist named Luitpold Sachse. He was one of a party of four prospectors who were working gold pockets of the Luangwa River about one hundred miles west of Lake Nyasa in Northern Rhodesia. They moved upstream from pocket to pocket in the hope of tracking down the source of the river gold. I had freighted in their equipment and sixteen natives and had agreed to stay on as meat hunter.

Sachse, who had studied at Columbia University, spoke English well. He knew nothing of hunting and said he had never shot even a BB gun. One morning I took him out after meat. Sixteen Kaffirs and five whites ate one hundred pounds of antelope a day.

Meat hunting isn't so simple as it sounds. Natives will eat anything in the meat line, but whites demand tasty flesh. Only a few African antelope are considered "white man's food." Most palatable is the klipspringer, a little forty-pound antelope that haunts the hills. This type is bagged only occasionally, consequently considered a dainty.

Next in preference is the five-hundred-pound

sable antelope, whose flesh is delicious. After sable, the next preference is the hartebeest, with duikerbok, impala (springbok), and bushbuck close behind. Waterbuck flesh is unchewable even when pounded to shreds. Puku meat is eaten only when no other is available. Flesh of most other types of antelope is either too strong or too insipid. Few white men care much for buffalo or wildebeest meat. Most, however, enjoy young zebra.

While describing problems of meat hunting to Sachse that torrid, breezeless morning, we came across Lichtenstein hartebeest sign in the center of a wide, treeless glade. I said:

"This dung was dropped about an hour ago. The bull's tracks are four inches from point to heel. That means he's upward of four hundred pounds. Looks like there are four cows with him." I pointed to a fringe of trees a half mile toward the river and said: "There's lion or leopard over there."

"Some connection?" Sachse asked.

"Well, normally hartebeest stay in shade during the heat of the day. They're not likely to come way out here in the broiling sun unless frightened." I back-spoored a little. "Notice how the tracks lead in a straight line from those trees up to here, and how they begin to curve now toward those bushes yonder? I think we'll find our game over there."

"Like a detective book," Sachse said.

"They've probably spotted us," I said, "but they're sometimes stupid. Maybe we can bag one."

Moving slowly, we angled toward the grove of bushes and entered about five hundred yards from where I thought the herd might be.

"Don't talk," I cautioned. "Don't step before feeling with your foot for twigs and stones. Don't cough. When I lift my hand—freeze."

Step by step, we went forward, standing for long minutes every few yards to watch for the flick of a tail or ear. We moved about three hundred yards in the next half hour, and I was beginning to think my guess hadn't been so hot when Sachse walked face-first into a thorn branch and said: "Ouch!"

Hartebeest exploded almost under our toes. There was no chance for a bullet close behind the foreleg—a shot that almost always drops a hartebeest—so I let a small cow have it through the belly. Of all antelopes, the hartebeest slows quickest from such a shot. The cow faltered before she had gone an eighth of a mile. She staggered a little, then stopped with head hanging. I moved up within 150 yards, lay down, and dropped her with a head shot.

Sachse wondered why I hadn't shot the bull; the bull had nice horns. I told him he'd enjoy cow meat much more than bull meat. I also pointed out that, although the bull was a large one, his horns weren't more than sixteen inches. Unless a Lichtenstein's horns measure at least nineteen and one half inches on the front curve, they aren't considered a worthwhile trophy.

That night as we sat around the fire puffing our pipes Sachse said:

"I've always thought of hunting as a rather low sport. You know, killing and all. But something's happened since our experience this morning. I find I've a strong urge to hunt. Fact is, I'd like to take over your job as meat hunter." He seemed embarrassed.

"Suits me," I said.

"Can you teach me? I mean, to shoot and all?"

"Sure."

"Take long?"

"Depends on you."

He turned to his partners, who were staring at him quizzically. "Sounds funny, I guess, but this morning was a revelation to me—stories in tracks, and all that. Fascinating. Makes geology seem tasteless. You fellows mind if I try it on?"

"Go ahead," they said. "Butcher Sachse," added one of the three, laughing.

I said: "True hunting is never butchery. It's almost one hundred percent sportsmanship. A true hunter has a sympathetic bond with animals. He tries to kill quickly and cleanly and never permits a wounded animal to suffer for long. Just now Sachse spoke of an 'urge' to hunt. Shows he's normal. Hunting's an atavistic urge and usually a healthy one. Of course there are perverted humans who kill game from sadistic motives or from blood lust. Such men kill from any spot where they feel safe—from trucks, jeeps, or tree platforms. They kill lion with dogs and run giraffe down with motorcars. Those men are not hunters."

"What got you all worked up?" someone asked. "Nobody's denying anything."

"Well," I said, "between 'butchers' and animals, I'm all for the animals."

Sachse said: "You fellows know I've always been a nature lover. That's one reason I'm hunting gold with you. But this morning while we were after that hartebeest I suddenly became aware of what someone has called 'strange, moody, broody' Africa. It began, I think, by the fact that we were hunting. When we stopped to take a breather in the shade of a tree, I lay flat, ear to the ground, and I swear I heard the sounds of grasses growing. I even thought I heard worms chewing their way through the dark and beetles digging graves for their prey. In other words, I became aware of life—unseen life—everywhere, in a new, deep way."

One man snorted.

"I know what Sachse means," I said. "Have you ever sat beside a stream and watched its border of reeds tremble and quiver as wild pigs, baby crocs, frogs, and otters, all unseen, wriggled and twisted down in the shadow?

"There's more quiet pleasure in one week of hunting antelope than in a whole season of big-game shooting. First, there's usually no hurry. The game will be waiting for you today, tomorrow, or the next day. In the meantime, there are mirages to marvel at, and brilliant birds. There are odors of spices, the cinnamon perfume of lilies, pungent sap from broken branches, the delightful stink of dung; sweet smells and sour smells. Each odor arouses memories of far years and far places."

"I saw a bird yesterday," Sachse said. "Its long tail streamed behind as it beat its wings in a hopeless effort to make headway against the wind. Suddenly the bird tipped, turned, and scudded away like a darting flower."

"Let's turn in," one of the partners said.

I shook out my blanket, wrapped it around me, and lay down, feet to the fire. Sachse stared moodily into the coals.

"Don't let those guys get you down, Sachse," I told him. "A hunter is always a poet—in his heart, at least."

Next morning Sachse began his lessons with the rifle.

There's little point in long, wearing hours of spooring and stalking if, after running down quarry, your shots miss. At more than two hundred yards you can't shoot accurately even with modern flat-trajectory bullets unless you can estimate distances to targets."

On the high veldt and in the back country, *first-time hunters almost always underestimate distances.*

That first day out with Sachse I would move away about fifty yards and tell him to catch, or at least get under, a tennis ball I'd throw toward him in a high arc. He'd reach for the ball, only to have it drop ten yards beyond him. Sometimes fifteen or more throws are required before a man learns to allow for deception caused by clear, light air.

I set up a six-foot-square target at two hundred yards and kept Sachse at it until shooting prone, he could group ten shots in an eight-inch area. It isn't hard to teach the average man to hold a rifle comfortably, keep sights upright, squeeze the trigger, and not flinch when letting off shots. A few men I've taught who seemed unable to stop bobbing and flinching were cured when I got them to use a smaller-caliber rifle. Sometimes an inch or so longer gunstock does the trick.

From single shots, still prone, I advanced Sachse to three rapid, trying to get all three off in twelve seconds. They had to be aimed shots and grouped within twelve inches. Most men learn rapid fire better with bolt-action rifles.

From prone we went to kneeling position and finally to standing. Then we moved the target to five hundred yards and went through the whole procedure again, attempting to get the prone group into a twenty-four-inch area. This rifle practice consumed about a week.

Evenings I'd show Sachse life-size drawings of various animal tracks, pointing out differences. The drawings were grouped, similar tracks overlaying one another in different colored inks.

For instance, tracks of kudu, sable, roan, and some hartebeests are much the same size and shape. When overlaid, the differences pop out like coal dust on snow. Eland and buffalo have spoor about the same size. Novices often confuse them.

Reedbuck, springbok, and puku have tracks very similar. In fact, old professionals sometimes have difficulty distinguishing between reedbuck and springbok spoor. Some find it hard to distinguish between the spoor of oribi and that of the common duiker.

Tracks of lion, leopard, elephant, giraffe, wildebeest, rhino, hippo, hyena, klipspringer, Tommy gazelle, and zebra are so distinctive that anyone can easily identify them. Novices sometimes confuse bush-pig and wart-hog spoor.

By the time Sachse had memorized the pictured characteristics of various tracks and was feeling quite cocky about it, he discovered that in practice he would seldom see a perfect hoof- or paw-print; that he'd have to judge most tracks from the points or heels only; and that in many cases he'd be able to identify a print only after removing dirt or sand that had fallen into it. He learned to remove such dirt with a feather.

I showed him how hooves of running antelope splay out; how tracks sheltered from wind and dust appear fresher than unsheltered ones. He learned to clear away matted grass and leaves and find prints in the ground below. I taught him about dropped leaf and grass chewings, scratches on bare rocks, displaced stones, and how to squint his eyes to prevent blurring in brilliant light. He absorbed knowledge like a sponge and was able, within three weeks, to locate and to follow reasonably distinct spoor.

However, finding and following spoor are not sufficient. One must know how fresh it is. Even old hands sometimes cannot determine this from tracks alone. But there's another sign of freshness that seldom fails. Dung!

A book could be written about game droppings. No two kinds of African animals have dung exactly alike, although manures of roan and sable antelope differ only in size. Moisture content is the best indication of the age of dung, and weather must be taken into consideration. The condition of grasses struggling whitely beneath old droppings can reveal the very day on which those droppings fell.

As I explained to Sachse, verbal and written descriptions of dungs are of little help. Even pictures tell a poor story. To learn about dungs, one has to see actual droppings.

Usually the eland, sable, and roan antelope leave single horselike droppings. Waterbuck droppings are somewhat similar but occasionally fall in clumps of three, four, or five. Kudu droppings are usually single and have small points on one end. Bushbuck deposits are oblong and wafflelike but sometimes break into little balls.

One day I said to Sachse: "Spooring can involve what one *doesn't* see even more than what one *does* see. It also involves sign that seems unnatural or misplaced. The depth of a toe point sometimes tells whether the animal was frightened or was merely running for the hell of it. Terrain frequently tells where game is heading. Spooring means leaving a lost trail, moving forward, and crisscrossing the area to find the tracks again. But most of all, spooring requires knowledge of animal habits so the tracker will know *why* and *where* the animals are doing what they are."

Sachse said: "You spoke of unnatural or misplaced sign. I don't get it."

To illustrate, I told him how ordinary cow dung once helped me locate the grave of a man who had been murdered, and how a wasps' nest, unnaturally fastened in a tree, led me to the hidden letter for which that man had been killed.

Here's the tale:

One October during my earlier African career, as I prepared to leave Tsumeb in Damaraland for a hunting trip above Matambanja in southeast Angola, a Major Gordon, British Intelligence officer, asked me if on my way I'd stop at Ian McKinnon's trading post and pick up an "important paper."

I surmised that the paper had to do with the slave trade. Renegade whites and Arabs even today run slaves up through Ethiopia to Red Sea ports. McKinnon was an old, old man, religious and dead set against slavers.

At the trading post a Cockney who introduced himself as Limey Scoggins greeted me by saying: "Mac's gone off on a trip. I'm in charge 'ere."

"How long's Mac been gone?"

"A few days."

"Too bad. I haven't seen him for two years. Where's his Hottentot boy, Sekomi? He'll help me get settled."

"Sekomi went with Mac. Sorry, sir, but you'd better not stay 'ere. Mac might not like it."

I laughed and motioned Ubusuku to set up my tent about one hundred yards west of Mac's two-room corrugated-iron quarters.

Scoggins shrugged and walked away.

I called after him: "How long did Mac say he'd be gone, Scoggins? "

Scoggins didn't answer. I watched him as he plodded toward the store. I figured Mac must have been up against it to have hired a man like the Cockney.

I helped Ubusuku finish tightening the tent, then said: "Scout around among the Kaffirs and find out what's been going on."

He returned shortly to say there wasn't a native on the place. "All gone," he said.

I checked the magazine of my .303, tucked it under my arm, and went to look around. Mac's cow, a big rawboned red-and-white beast, lay under a mimosa tree at the edge of the clearing, chewing her cud and scratching her back with long horns. Something about her aroused my spooring instincts. Something wasn't quite right. I'd been a hunter for too long to shrug the "feeling" off. I tried the old trick of looking at things from the side of my eye. Corners of the eyes often see things that direct gaze misses.

The sense of something haywire was strongest when I looked at the cow. She seemed completely bored. With eyes shut, she chewed slowly and listlessly. I stalked across to the front of Mac's store. I banged on the sill of the Dutch door. Scoggins opened it and I stepped inside.

"I don't see any of Mac's Kaffirs around," I said.

"They went with 'im."

"You're alone here?"

"Not a soul 'ere but me. Glad you popped along. Company, that's wot you'll be."

"Where did Mac say he was going?"

" 'E just said 'upcountry.' 'E was worried-like."

I stared. Scoggins flushed and said: "That's wot Mac said. I'm telling you wot 'e said. I don't know another bloody thing."

I looked about the room. Strips of hippo hide hung from a wire. Lion and leopard skins were piled on the floor. Shelves held bolts of bright calico, jars of beads, and spools of copper wire for making bangles. There were canned fruits and vegetables. I pushed past Scoggins into Mac's bedroom. The cot was neatly made. Clothes hung on wall pegs. Then I noticed Mac's Bible, face down, leaves crumpled, on the floor in a corner. It was a pocket Bible, and I knew Mac never went anywhere without it. I knew, too, that Mac revered his Bible so much that he wouldn't even place another book on top of it.

I left the Bible where it was, but began to fear that Mac was dead. I said:

"Scoggins, I'll stick around till Mac gets back if you don't mind."

"Why should I mind?"

"Just an expression," I said. "But on second thought, I probably won't stay. Mac may be away too long."

I saw Scoggins relax. He said: "Myke y'rself at 'ome just like Mac was 'ere."

"Nice of you," I said, and walked out.

In the tent I wrote a hasty note to the district *chefe de posto,* who I hoped would be at Bambe, about 150 miles northwest. Knowing the laxness of Portuguese officials in Angola, I took a long chance and said I'd found MacKinnon's body. I hoped that would bring the *chefe de posto* on the run.

I gave the message to Ubusuku, who would make the 150 miles in two days. Seventy-five miles a day was duck soup for that lad. How long it would take the *chefe de posto* and his squad of native soldiers was hard to say.

After Ubusuku had gone, I got the willies. If Scoggins had killed Mac, he'd probably try to kill me. I went into the woods to do some thinking. I followed a faint trail that obviously led to the river. A quarter of a mile along, that odd hunch of something wrong again assailed me. As my eyes searched the trees around me, "something phony" seemed to smack me in the face. It was one of more than a score of wasps' nests in a thorn tree. It was exactly like the others, except that instead of being cemented to a twig it hung from a thorn.

No untrained eye would have seen anything unusual about that nest, but to a hunter's eyes, the nest stood out like a warship in a glass of water. I hooked the nest down with a stick, broke it open, and found a rolled envelope wrapped in glassine cloth. I unrolled it. The upper left corner read: "On His Majesty's Service." It was addressed to an official in the South African Constabulary.

I was sure now that Mac was dead and that he had had a hunch he might be killed. He had hidden the envelope on the river trail, knowing some old hunting hand would spot it someday.

I put the envelope back in the glassine and buried it off the trail. Then, deeply troubled, I walked back to the clearing.

As I crossed diagonally toward my tent, I noticed several round, whitish spots from which cow flops had been lifted. At first I assumed Mac's Kaffirs had been gathering dried dung for fires. Then my mind flashed to Mac's cow. The "something haywire" about the cow was no longer a mystery.

I recalled clearly that the cow had been lying near a scattering of cow flops. *Some dried-out flops had overlapped moist ones.* For eleven days I did little but walk through the woods in fuming

Eland bull.

impatience. Scoggins kept busy at the post store, "cleaning 'ouse against Mac's return," he said. I knew, of course, that he was searching the building for the missing envelope.

The twelfth day, exactly at noon, the *chefe de posto* and his party, led by Ubusuku, entered the clearing. Scoggins stuck his head out through the Dutch door.

"Wot th' bloody 'ell!" he said.

Mac's body was found in a shallow grave beneath the cow flops. He hadn't even been wrapped in a blanket.

Scoggins had been hired to steal the envelope by a Kurd slaver named Aliche; he had killed Mac by choking him. Before burying Mac's body, he had paid the Kaffirs off and sent them to their homes. When he noticed fresh manure on the grave, he got the idea that additional dry cow flops would indicate the ground hadn't been disturbed for a long time.

As I ended the McKinnon story, Sachse said: "Interesting. According to your theory, spooring is chiefly deductive reasoning."

"Partly."

"To make accurate presuppositions about animals' actions, one would have to know their habits and behavior patterns. Right?"

"Let's not get collegiate," I said. "You merely have to know a lot about animals."

Sachse was silent for a time. Then he said: "I think I understand now that the true value of a game trophy lies in the experience of acquiring it rather than in its rarity or size. I don't think I'll go back to Switzerland."

"No?"

"No. I think I'll stay in Africa to become a professional hunter."

He did. For almost thirty years Luitpold Sachse roamed most of Africa with his camera and his gun.

Corel Professional Photos CD-ROM

Springbuck

13

MORE ANTELOPE

ALTHOUGH YOU go to Africa with the idea of shooting big game only, chances are you'll spend ninety per cent of your time hunting antelope. And the longer you hunt them, the more you'll enjoy it.

It takes a he-man to be a successful antelope hunter. You'll likely walk twenty-five miles for each shot fired. You'll find antelope in twos, threes, and small herds; will never see those "moving-picture" herds containing thousands of animals except in some game preserve.

You'll walk on ground so hot you'll have to take off your boots occasionally to cool your feet; or in weather so damp and cold that ticks under your shirt curl up and drop off. You'll sweat or you'll shiver. Your hands will be cut by saw-toothed grass. Spear grass will punch little holes in your flesh. You'll get tangled in reeds, bogged in marsh, dunked in rivers, and you'll itch and scratch and blister.

Your rifle barrel will get so hot that you can't hold your hand on it, or it'll be so cold it'll feel like an icicle. The gun that seemed so light and easily handled during the first hour of the day will seem to grow heavier and heavier. If you've loaded your bandoleer or pouches with too many cartridges, their weight will drag at you. You'll feel like tossing many away—and probably will.

Unless you've been on a good meat diet and eaten your food well salted, you'll find yourself strangely weak and listless when energy is most needed. If you're a man who lives exclusively on fruits, vegetables, and grains, chances are you won't be able to endure a prolonged African hunting trip. Africa's a land of "lazy," listless, easily tired natives because it's a land where natives get little meat. Millions of natives go through life with little meat in their diets because they raise no cattle and live in areas where game is scarce.

Any old-time hunter will tell you that when a group of Kaffirs is first hired they're usually a miserable, easily fagged lot. After two or three feeds of meat—any kind—they become cheerful, energetic, and enthusiastic.

I've never liked the Masai of Kenya and Tanganyika. They're cocky, too assured of their own superiority over anybody, white or black. But the Masai can do more sustained work, endure longer periods of hunting, and suffer less fatigue than any tribe in Africa. Every morning at milking time they tap the veins of their cattle (every man has a good-size herd), mix blood with the milk, and drink about three pints. No fruits. No vegetables. No grains.

Practically next door to the Masai live the Kikuyu and the Wakamba, vegetarians of necessity. They're disease-ridden, dull, and without stamina. Under pressure of a tough hunt they become sullen and uncooperative. But feed them a heavy meat diet and they become keen, vigorous, and eager to please.

I know from experience that unless a hunter gets lots of mineral salts and meat proteins (vegetable and grain proteins are not sufficient) he breaks down under difficult going. When he *does* get those salts and proteins, he takes hardships in his stride.

Lester Fletcher was a vegetarian from Zion City, Illinois. He suffered from sinus trouble and general debilitation. He had been told by a physician that he needed a hunting trip. With him he brought cereals, fruits, vegetables, and "health" foods. He chewed each mouthful so long that the food slipped down his throat, he said, without swallowing.

We camped in the Enkeldoorn district of Mashonaland. On the first day out after springbok we had not gone five miles when Fletcher broke into a cold sweat and became so weak that he had to be carried into shade by the Kaffirs. I gave him a "homemade" salt pill and a big drink of boiled water. He shivered with chill for about twenty minutes, then fell asleep. After the nap he got back to camp under his own power and went directly to his cot. I broiled an antelope steak on a stick at the open fire, salted it, and offered it to him. He turned his head away in disgust.

For a week Fletcher went through the same daily fiasco. On Sunday afternoon, after watching him munch away, I said:

"Look, Fletcher, either you begin eating meat or we go back to Bulawayo. Right now your resistance is so low I expect any minute to see you down with fever. I don't want you dying on my hands."

The word "fever" did it. He was scared. The man deserves credit, for he probably never swallowed anything for which he had more aversion than the piece of springbok liver I toasted for him. He gagged several times, finally got it down, then said, "I'm sick," and lay down under a wagon.

For supper that night we had a haunch of antelope that had been baked for twelve hours in a mud blanket. Fletcher was dozing when I began breaking the mud with blows from my knife handle. Steam squirted from the first crack. A breeze carried the aroma to Fletcher. He rolled from under the wagon bed and sat up, sniffing.

He ate that meal like a Kaffir and drank three mugs of tea. From then on he ate meat daily and within three weeks was doing twenty-five to thirty miles a day. The meek, Milquetoast character of that first day's safari had become a hard-muscled, hearty eater and sound sleeper. Even the sinus trouble disappeared.

African antelope are said to be the hardiest game animals on earth. Many of them, when wounded anywhere in the body except lungs or heart, get away. Hardiest of all are the little common duikerbok and the big waterbuck. These can carry an awful lot of lead. They often go fifty to one hundred yards with a slug through the heart or through both lungs. Others exceptionally hard to kill are the hartebeest, wildebeest, red lechwe, puku, and sassaby.

A mistake many sportsmen make in hunting antelope is that they fail to plan for a good collection of horns and accept any beast that comes along. Nothing lets a man down more than having a taxidermist look down his nose at trophies because the horns are less than average length.

I saved a lot of unnecessary hunting by asking clients about the rooms in which they intended hanging trophies. I'd have them draw diagrams showing proportions of spaces on walls and suggest something like this:

"A kudu head here, a sable there, an impala at this spot, a duikerbok at that, buffalo over the mantel, wildebeest opposite, eland below the kudu, roan below the sable."

Then, when the sportsman had decided on the heads he really wanted, we'd go after them, bagging only beasts with horns well above average and always keeping eyes peeled for a record pair.

There are rules for sensible, safe hunting of antelope just as there are for big game. A man who violates the rules takes a chance on being killed, hooked, knifed with hoofs, or trampled, particularly by wounded sable, roan, or gemsbok.

Dr. Sidney Woburn whipped his rifle to his shoulder and fired as a big, solitary sable bull we had been trailing suddenly stood out in strong silhouette against a background of gray-green brush. The bull collapsed, legs under him, neck outstretched. He seemed to be a very extinct antelope.

For a few moments we stood admiring the beast's beautifully curved horns. Then Woburn moved closer, and thinking he was going to use his knife to make sure the animal was dead, I handed my rifle to a camp boy. Woburn yelled. I whirled just in time to see him knocked flat by a flashing sweep of the bull's horns. The sable was on his knees, struggling vainly to lift his hindquarters. I grabbed for my .303, but before I could shoot, the grunting bull again hooked at Woburn, the point of one horn slashing the slack of Doc's shirt. It was a close shave. Death missed Doc by an inch.

My shot back of the eye finished the sable but ruined the head. I hadn't dared take a chance on a shot anywhere else.

In months following, Doc got a fine collection of heads, but never again did he get close to even a klipspringer without making sure it was dead. The knife-sharp hoofs of even the little antelope can rip a man open as neatly as those of the big ones.

Many sportsmen cherish memories of nights about the fires far more than the memories of actual hunting. With pipes going and flames driving back the chill; with firelight pushing shadows back against Africa's mysterious darkness; with the sense of well-being that follows a hard-earned meal, men become talkative.

They discuss the luck of the day and hopes for tomorrow. They spin yarns of their own, then turn to the white hunter for tales of strange treks and strange peoples.

I'd tell my parties odd bits about animals they were likely to run across. Maybe I'd seen steinbok and duikerbok spoor that day. I'd say something like this:

"Frightened steinbok bound away so fast that it's

almost impossible to hit one with a rifle. Duikerbok run thirty or forty yards, stop, and then look back. Plenty of time for an aimed shot. Oribi, reedbuck, and some of the hartebeests also pause and look back. However, almost all antelope, if not chased, will stop well out of range and turn around to see what had frightened them."

Sometimes we'd stage question and answer shows:

Why do you say that eland spoor is easy to follow?

They're heavy animals, with front feet larger than back ones.

You speak of "blue" eland and "red" eland. How come?

"Blue" are old elands. They're almost hairless and gray-blue. Younger elands are reddish with darker necks and backs.

Is it true that sitatunga dive under water to eat grasses from river bottoms?

I've never seen them do it, but natives swear it's true. Sitatunga spend much time in bogs, marshes, and water. Their hoofs spread wide, making easy going in soft ground. I've gotten my best sitatunga bags from boats. Lechwe also live in boggy, wet areas.

Which is the most common antelope?

Hartebeest.

Which are hardest to stalk?

On plains, I think the springbok are hardest. Seldom get within five hundred yards of them. If you have cover, though, they're no harder to stalk than other antelope. In brush I think the bushbuck's hardest.

Such sessions brought out much miscellaneous information:

Puku are comparatively easy to stalk. Bushbuck lurk in dense brush during the heat of the day. They come into more open country early mornings and late evenings. When frightened, they bark. Gerenuk and klipspringers require only the water supplied by dew on the grass. Gerenuk often browse while standing on their hind legs. Each of the fourteen species of hartebeest has differently shaped horns on their horse-faced heads.

Zebras seem always to be taking off in a cloud of dust and frightening the animals you're stalking. Reedbuck warn other antelope of a hunter by making high-pitched bleats. A wound that would merely slow a duikerbok would kill a reedbuck. When frightened, springbok usually give a single bark and jump high. Each individual jumps in the direction he's heading, so they often crash into one another in mid-air. Because of their graceful horns and rich, warm, chestnut coats, springbok are most admired of all antelope.

Wildebeests are generally brown with a bluish tinge, but color varies. When wounded, they sometimes play dead until the hunter gets close, then leap up, bowl the hunter over, and gallop away. The sassabies can run faster and farther than other antelope. They're found chiefly in northeast Rhodesia.

Kudu die from wounds that would not be fatal to some of their tougher kindred. In a poll of fifty-five sportsmen taken in Nairobi one season, kudu horns were adjudged the finest in Africa. I think that sable horns are superior to those of kudu when vewed form the side. The spread of kudu horns between points has much to do with their desirability. Hunters always hope to find a kudu with a spread of forty-eight inches.

Tourist hunters seem surprised to discover that most professional white hunters are also ardent game conservationists who often wax profane over laws that permit needless slaughter of animals. Because of the meat hunger undermining the health of natives all over Africa, the government of Tanganyika permits native blacks to carry "gas-pipe" guns and for about fifteen cents a year licenses them to shoot unlimited game *for their own consumption*. A beneficent idea, but is doesn't work.

Reason: Tanganyika is East Indian country. There are 46,000 Indians as against about 16,000 whites. East Indians, as much "foreigners" as are whites, control almost all housing and the largest share of all business. *They also direct the largest game-animal bootleg industry in the world.*

Old hunters estimate that each year, from Tanganyika native blacks, Indians buy the meat, skins, ivory, tails, and horns of at least 190,000 game animals. Natives want money more than they want meat, and the Indians see that they get it, knowing they'll quickly get it back again.

White hunters insist that for every beast killed outright by natives, two are wounded and left to be devoured by lions, hyenas, wild dogs, vultures, and ants. Natives simply cannot learn to shoot well, and even an expert rifleman would find it difficult to kill cleanly with one of the antique muzzle-loaders used by natives.

For years Rhodesia slaughtered tens of thousands of game animals annually in the mistaken idea that it would this eliminate the tsetse fly. Hunting licenses in Rhodesia are nominal in price. In Northern Rhodesia you can get a complete bag of game animals, pay for transportation and native trackers at a cost not much more than the price of a full license alone in Kenya.

There is, in East Africa, another game menace, one that knows no mercy or sportsmanship. It's the Boer "driedmeat hunter" who annually invades game country and kills thousands of antelope, sun-dries the flesh, loads it into trucks, and goes home with a year's supply for families and native hands.

No one knows how many animals these vandals kill, but one ton of biltong represents about 130 dead springbok or 45 dead hartebeests.

Unhappily, many old-fashioned Boers seem entirely lacking in sportsmanship. They control their natives by vicious beatings and permit them fewer privileges than they permit their animals. They're butchers who seldom select an individual animal for a shot, but blaze away at a herd, wounding or maiming five for every one killed. Somehow these old Boers gained reputation as excellent riflemen. Yet many shoot atrociously. They seldom attempt to run down a wounded animal unless it's so badly hurt that the chase won't be long.

Kenya authorities sometimes pursue biltong hunters for hundreds of miles, arrest them, and bring them to trial. Getting convictions, however, isn't always easy. In any case, the number arrested are so few as to be negligible. There aren't enough game wardens to make a dent in the traffic.

Of all game-country governments, that of Kenya is most conservation-conscious. A full license permitting the killing of 99 animals costs a visitor-hunter the equivalent of $180. License for a single elephant costs S140, and license for a second elephant within the year costs an additional $280.

Many of the 99 animals are included in the list only so hunting parties may kill for meat. Here's the full license list:

One each of: blue monkey, bongo, cheetah, Kenya oribi, Haggard's oribi, klipspringer, Chanler's reedbuck, sitatunga, Jackson's hartebeest, Hunter's antelope, callotis oryx, ellipsoprymnus waterbuck, defassa waterbuck, roan, sable, greater kudu (male head only and taken only in Turkana or Northwest Frontier District), eland, Grevy's zebra, hippo (but only within five miles of Lake Victoria), lion, leopard.

Two each of: Peter's gazelle.

Three each of: pygmy antelope, gerenuk, impala (springbok), Coke's hartebeest, topi, beisa oryx, wildebeest, buffalo, steinbok.

Four each of: Grant's gazelle, bohor reedbuck, lesser kudu, common zebra.

Six each of: bushbuck, oribi (but not Haggard's or Kenya variety), duikerbok, dik-dik.

Nine each of: Thompson's gazelle.

For the sportsman in a hurry there's a two-week license costing $42. It permits one each of buffalo, pygmy antelope, steinbok, gerenuk, common zebra, lesser kudu, Grant's gazelle, bohor reedbuck, springbok, Coke's hartebeest, wildebeest, topi, beisa oryx; two each of bushbuck, dik-dik, oribi, duikerbok; three of Thompson's gazelle.

In the Congo, except for gorillas, game-law enforcement is comparatively lax mainly because the territory is too large to police. Here and in Angola natives work in cahoots with game bootleggers, and slaughter is outrageous.

Americans take quite a beating in Africa from sportsmen of other nationalities because of America's insane slaughter of bison and carrier pigeons and because American fur buyers are today responsible for the near-extinction of the African leopard. Not only do fur merchants' representatives encourage illegal trapping, particularly in Ethiopia, but they also manufacture the traps.

Sportsmanship of American hunters visiting Africa improves each year. Where once they often were boastful, swaggering, roistering, wild-shooting characters, they're now chiefly men educated in matters of conservation.

In time one can learn all about big game, but a lifetime is too short to really know the multitude of African antelope. There are scores of subspecies. Some are seldom mentioned in print, others seldom mentioned outside Africa. Among the latter are the bulbul, lelwel, bontebok, twenty-five of the thirty-four species of duikerbok, sunis dwarf antelope, royal antelope, Vaal rhebok, debatog, addax, and the recently extinct blaubok.

Hunting antelope is indeed a he-man sport. It can take you from Cape to Cairo and from Mombasa to Sierra Leone. Your bag, if you wish, can include scores of different-type animals ranging from the pretty little ten-inch-at-the-shoulder royal antelope of Nigeria to the six-foot-high sable of East Africa.

Then there's the okapi, usually called an antelope, but a member of the giraffe family. The okapi is the rarest of all African animals. He is purple-skinned, with white-barred legs, and ears like a mule. He's a gentle, timid animal averaging 250 pounds when full grown. A live one is worth $6000. There are only seven of them in the zoos of the world.

The okapi is found only in the rain forests of the Congo and is never found in pairs. They are a government monopoly, and the only person permitted to trap them is Captain Jean de Medina, *chef du groupe de capture et d'elevage d'okpis.*

I've never shot an okapi and have seen only two wild ones. However, my hunting partner, Miki Carter, of Los Gatos, California, one of the world's best big-game cameramen, was in on the capture of an adult and a newborn okapi in 1952. Miki got a picture of the little week-old calf—the first ever captured alive—as it was brought into camp on the shoulders of pygmies.

Better not try hunting okapis unless you're prepared to spend some time in a Congo jail. If you want to get in on a capture, make arrangements with Captain de Medina. Write him at the Government Elephant Farm at Andudu.

Memories of hardships while antelope hunting grow dim, but memories of days like happy songs grow always clearer. Cool, dewy mornings under cloudless sky. Brush-rimmed glades at midmorning like sleeping, golden veldt-grass pools; midday with heat mirage flowing gently; late afternoons alive with insect whisperings and the noiseless rush of the sun down the last miles of the sky.

Shadows tiptoeing out from under the feet of the brush, reaching eastward slowly and cautiously overlaying the gold of the grasses with purples and lavenders. The pair of roan antelope whose spoor had led to them stepping daintily into the open, keeping on the dark side of the lengthening bush shadows, the more venturesome reddish-roan female slightly ahead of the bluish-roan male.

Abruptly they step confidently into the sunlight and by some quirk of light rays appear almost white. A faint sound from behind, and a turn of the head reveals a *lagavaan* rousing himself from sleep. Sluggishly, he breaks from the shadowed coolness into the sun's warmth, and for a few moments the ugly five-foot lizard glimmers with iridescent silvers and blues. He shifts positions slightly and his beauty vanishes.

The roans walk away at an angle. I estimate the value of the male's horns and judge them worthwhile. I lift my rifle, and the buck stands to give a perfect quartering shot. I sigh and lower the muzzle.

Well, *lagavaans* are good eating. I turn and aim at the lizard, but remember his vagrant flashing colors and take my finger from the trigger. Disgusted with my softness, I give him a light thump on the back with the butt of the gun. The *lagavaan* opens his mouth as if laughing.

Oh well, there'll be shooting tomorrow.

14

LEOPARDS

POUND FOR POUND, the African leopard is the strongest, fightingest animal on earth. His strength is fantastic. He can hang an antelope *three times* his own weight, twenty feet up in a tree. I once watched a 100-pound leopard disembowel a sassaby antelope, drag the 240-pound carcass 300 yards, lug it fifteen feet up into a wild fig tree, and hang it by the neck from a crotch.

If a 125-pound leopard were double in weight he could subdue the 500-pound lion, the 1,500-pound buffalo; play havoc with large antelope such as eland, roan, sable, and wildebeest; drag the Nile crocodile from water by its nose; and destroy any unarmed man who dared face him.

Leopards, both black and spotted, are smarter and more vicious than lions. Once he begins a fight, the leopard battles to the death. Not so the lion, who quits when odds are against him. When a lion has defeated his enemy his blood lust vanishes; but the leopard's hatred continues until he's torn the guts from his victim, human or animal.

Leopards live everywhere in Africa; on the plains, in wooded *kloofs,* on mountain slopes, in brush and forest. While I was writing this book, a leopard was reported to have been killed within forty miles of Johannesburg, a city of more than 650,000 persons. Because of heavy demand for skins, particularly in America, leopards are nearing extinction in certain areas, but until Africa's last wooded section and brush-grown ravine are cleared, leopards will survive.

Leopards are sneaky, treacherous, and fast. Many professional hunters have never seen one in daytime. Others have seen only flashes as the beasts slipped behind cover. On the other hand, a good leopard hunter sees them during both days and nights because he knows where to look for them. In 1921 between the Ganale Dorya and Webbe rivers in Gallaland, I shot eleven leopards in thirty-five days. An Ethiopian princeling, Ras Kassai, paid five pounds for each skin—fifty-five pounds in all.

But that was only the beginning of the deal. In most of Ethiopia, salt and cartridges are used for money. Men who amount to anything carry rifles—useless old shooting irons such as trade guns and bunged-up French Lebels. The rifles are carried as marks of distinction, like Englishmen's canes. No one ever thinks of trying to fire one.

The only coined money accepted by back-country Ethiopians is the Maria Theresa dollar. However, cartridges will buy anything, including land and cattle. I took my fifty-five pounds to an Arab money merchant and traded them for Maria Theresa dollars. With those I bought blocks of salt. I sold the salt for cartridges and traded the cartridges for Maria Theresa dollars. Back in Harrar, I exchanged the big silver dollars for 173 English pounds. Later, in Johannesburg, I exchanged the pounds for American gold at the rate of $4.82 per pound. Thus, with a little trading, my eleven leopard skins finally brought me $834, or about $76 each.

While the leopard prefers to stay as far from man as possible, there are times when he'll attack. Many a black spearman whose first thrust at a leopard was not fatal has ended with his bowels outside his body. A female leopard with cubs will not hesitate to attack if she thinks her babies are threatened. A leopard with painful wounds will sometimes attack with ferocity. Carl Akeley, famed American museum hunter, was once attacked by an eighty-pound leopard he had wounded in one foot. Here's the way he told me the story:

"It was dusk. I'd trailed the leopard to a small island in a river. She was little more than a dark shadow when I saw her about thirty yards from me. I fired. She rushed me and I found myself holding a clawing, biting demon in my arms. She set her jaws in my upper right forearm. I got my left hand on her throat. She chewed. Every time she'd relax her jaws to take another bite, I'd pull my arm through her teeth an inch or so. Finally she'd chewed down to my wrist and I got my fist in her mouth. Fortunately, her feet hung so low she couldn't get her claws into my belly.

"Bleeding, gasping, and straining, I used every ounce of strength in an effort to shut off her wind. She remained as strong as ever, and I lost hope. We fell to the ground—I on top. I got my elbows under her armpits and spread her forelegs so wide she couldn't claw me. I drew up my knees, placed them against her chest, and pushed. One of her ribs cracked. She relaxed slightly. Another rib cracked. I felt her weaken and began to hope that I might win. I shoved my fist farther into her throat. Slowly, she stopped struggling. I got to my feet, knifed her—and the battle was over.

"Back in camp, friends pumped antiseptic solution into my badly chewed arm. I got well because I was young and husky and could take it."

Leopards are not difficult to bag if you know their habits. They're suckers for traps, hesitating only briefly before entering a walk-in cage if the bait is tasty, such as young wild pig, monkey, kid, lamb, or antelope. Bait doesn't have to be live, for leopards are eaters of carrion. Most leopards are caught these days in American-made steel traps, a method that turns the stomachs of true sportsmen.

With a rifle, leopard hunting pays off in sustained excitement. As you follow his spoor there's always the chance he may be in the trees above you or lurking on top of a nearby anthill or rock, or even padding noiselessly behind you.

Leopards hunt alone. I've never seen two wild leopards together. In fact, I've never seen two within miles of each other. Many hunters have heard leopards mating, but I've never known a white man who's seen them mate. At mating times the male's a mean character, as yowls of the female testify.

Native hunters in Ethiopia, Uganda, and the

Camaroons have told me that sometimes two or three male leopards sit nearby and, as soon as a mating is over, pounce on the "husband" and give him a mauling. There must be some truth in this story, coming as it does from widely separated parts of the continent.

Four times I've seen baboons attack leopards. Once when a leopard had captured a young baboon, four adult male baboons killed the big cat in a matter of minutes. Another time I saw two baboons jump from a rock upon a leopard passing below, sever its jugular, tear open its bowels, and rush screaming up the hillside. In southern Uganda I watched three baboons lie in wait for a leopard that was sneaking belly-to-ground after a hare. When the stalking leopard passed, they hit him like a whirlwind. His hoarse, rasping grunts as he fought for life told of agony. The baboons left him in pieces. In Southern Rhodesia I saw five baboons rush down from a tree, hop and skip about in a frenzy, rush to the brink of a dry spruit, and leap on something below. They roared, barked, and shrieked. Two of the five scrambled back up and over the edge and raced past me without even seeing me. They were in a panic. Below, three baboons lay dead, two with broken backs and one slashed by teeth and claws. Tufts of bloody leopard hair were all about, but the leopard was nowhere to be seen.

Professionals use two methods of hunting leopards. One is to observe the leopard's route to and from his den when he goes on the prowl and ambush him along the way. The other is to wait near the den for a leopard's return from his hunt and bag him as he enters. Sounds simple, but there are complications.

The den is usually a cave high up on the face of a *krans*, or the slope of a hill. From the cave's mouth or from a rock or tree close by, the leopard can look out over terrain below. He'll lie for hours, head on paws or lifted in regal dignity, watching every movement and listening to every sound in the panorama below.

The largest leopard I ever shot weighed 145 pounds, measuring eight feet two inches from nose to tail tip, and standing two feet six inches at the shoulder. The average is about 85 pounds, six feet straight, and two feet two inches at the shoulder.

The occasion was in 1911 on one of my first transport-wagon trips with Nicobar Jones. I was eighteen, and the Zulu, Ubusuku, who had just become my tracker, was about twenty-two. We were outspanned this side of the hump in Portuguese East Africa (now Mozambique), about one hundred miles southwest of the Zambezi. Jones had sent us out to get an antelope or a couple of bustards for supper. We had picked up the spoor of a Lichtenstein's hartebeest and followed it into the wide mouth of a wooded *kloof.* We lost the trail and began searching the ground along a small, turbulent stream that came down from high slopes. Ubusuku grunted, and thinking he'd picked up the track, I went over to where he knelt on moist ground at the water's edge.

It was not antelope spoor, but the clear impression of four toe pads and the shamrock-shaped heel pad of a leopard. What a leopard! Instead of the average three and one-half inches from tip of largest toe to back of heel, this print measured five and one-quarter inches. For a moment I thought of lion spoor, but there was no mistaking the narrower paw mark of leopard.

We back-spoored and found a partial print and decided the leopard had been running toward the creek. The water was knee-deep, and we waded out to a rock in midstream. Puddles showed the big cat had been on the rock only a short time earlier. Ubusuku leaped from the rock to the farther bank and immediately signaled that the leopard had likewise made the jump and had headed upstream.

We surmised the beast's den was somewhere high along the *kloof* face, probably far back toward the summit. We were young and excitable. We would have gone after that leopard then and there had I not heard the sound of the hartebeest drinking downstream behind us. Automatically I wheeled and fired. The antelope dropped, half in water. The noise of the shot boomed and echoed through the hills, and we knew leopard hunting was over for that night.

Back at the outspan, we handed the liver, kidneys, heart, and four haunches of the hartebeest to the Kaffir cook, and with Ubusuku beside me to verify my story I described the big spoor to Jones. He said:

"That's an awful big print, but it could be."

"How about going after him tomorrow morning?" I asked.

Jones wrinkled his eyes, and his beard seemed to bristle. He said: "Gotta get over the hump before dark. We'll inspan early."

"But that leopard!"

"Neither of you's smart enough to bag a leopard—not yet."

"Maybe we'll be lucky," I said hopefully.

"Ain't no luck."

I turned away, disappointed. We ate supper in silence. Just before we crawled beside the oxen to sleep, Jones said:

"Get down by the spruit before sun-up. Lay for him where he landed from the rock. Get downwind and lay on your bellies. Don't talk. Wait two hours. If he don't come along, git on up the *kloof* and find where he holes up. Have to judge his cave by hair and spoor outside. Tigers [leopards], except females with cubs, don't take food into their sleeping place."

"Swell," I said. And before I dropped off to sleep I added: "Thanks, Mr. Jones."

But old Nicobar Jones was dead to the world.

He jerked my blanket off me an hour before sunrise. He called Ubusuku over from the Kaffirs' fire and said to us:

"If you go up the *kloof*, watch for game hangin' in a tree. A fellow as big as that one's been eatin' hearty a long time. Maybe he's got a tree he uses as a regular larder." He turned squarely to me and added: "You won't likely git more'n one shot at this cat. You know the rule."

I nodded. Jones raised his eyebrows.

"Keep calm and shoot straight," I said.

Jones grunted.

I ran the pull-through through my rifle, took the solid from the breech, and replaced it with a soft-nose. I checked the leaf sight and the magazine, put on the safety catch, and led the way through the knee-high wet grass. There was just enough light to see that our trail was a dark path behind us.

Almost at the spot where we had found the leopard's spoor I realized I had left camp without morning coffee for the first time in memory.

Sure, I was excited. So was Ubusuku. We crossed the creek, stepped into brush, and threaded our way downstream to a spot near the rock that the leopard had used as a stepping stone. Time after time we tested the air for a breeze. There was none. Ubusuku, naked except for shorts, lay on his belly, eyes half shut. Ants crawled over him. A long, green worm slowly inched the length of his back. A spider dropped to his thigh and ran across the bare brown skin. Ubusuku didn't twitch a muscle.

I lay, rifle beside me. An ant began dancing a jig on a spot below my belt. I scratched. Another ant raced on the skin of my stomach. Some sort of bug got under an armpit. I began itching all over, particularly between my toes. By the time the sun was well up, I was in misery. But I was proud of myself. I hadn't sneezed or moved except for that one scratch.

There had been no sign of the leopard, nor, for that matter, of any other animal. The brush was silent except for the flutter of birds and the cheepings of insects. I nudged Ubusuku and we walked silently along the bank toward the rock.

In the clear, cool water, nose pressed against the downstream side of the rock, was a fifteen-pound tiger fish, his orange fins and tail motionless except for slight quivering caused by the current. He was in shadow, but as we watched, sunlight was reflected from a white stone on the creek bottom and the big fish was suddenly iridescent.

Ubusuku leaped atop the rock and slowly lowered his hand into the water. Inch by inch he reached toward the drowsing tiger fish. I held my breath. Ubusuku turned his hand palm up and scratched the fish's belly. The fish opened its mouth as if grinning, showing long, ugly, wide-spaced teeth. Ubusuku kept on tickling. Little by little the dark brown hand moved toward the forepart of the fish. Then, with Ubusuku's first two fingers in a gill, the fish was out of water, throwing silver drops in all directions as he struggled for release. Ubusuku pierced the fleshless skull with knife point, and the beautiful fish, colors already fading, was still. We wrapped it in wet staghorn moss and an outer wrapping of leaves. We tied the bundle with clematis withes and hid it deep in a tree fern.

Then, with me in the lead, we started up the *kloof.*

For a while we followed close to the stream, but brush became so thick and tangled we had to twist, wind, push through curtains of branches, and crawl through holes in clematis-bound bushes. My rifle was a problem, and I finally took the cartridge from the chamber, grasped the muzzle, and dragged the gun on the ground behind me. Even then the leaf sight was pulled out of kilter.

Stones and thorns dug into my knees and the palms of my hands. My britches became so tight in the crotch I had difficulty in moving. I put my hand on a puffball, and fine, yellow dust spurted into my eyes and nose. I nearly smothered trying to keep from sneezing. By that time I don't think I'd have seen a leopard if it had been squatting in front of me. I motioned to Ubusuku to take the lead.

Almost at once he spotted leopard hair on the bark of a tree. He held the hair tightly in his closed hand and blew warm breath on it. He looked at it and whispered:

"New hair. Maybe yesterday."

In the gloom I couldn't even see the hair lying on his palm. Natives' eyes are much sharper than white men's, particularly at night. We proved that around campfires many times. When discussing eyesight, someone would take a few pins and toss them to the ground. The game was to see how many pins each white man could find in flickering firelight. Few pins were found. Then the Kaffirs would be called, pins thrown, and natives asked to pick them up. With little hesitation they'd find most of them.

The *kloof* widened at a spot where a waterfall sparkled as it fell into a perfectly round pool hollowed from solid rock. Wild fig trees pushed the brush back with gnarled arms. The ground cover of moss so red in the shade was faded and rusty in sunlight. Small gray monkeys with pert black faces and long tails chittered at us. Birds of many colors darted and wooped over the pool.

I took off my boots and let my hot feet soak up

coolness from the water. Ubusuku stood under the falling waters and his 195-pound, six-feet-four brown body turned to glistening, wet chocolate. The monkeys increased their shrill cursing. Then they were completely silent. I looked into the trees. The little rascals were gone.

It occurred to me that they might have been frightened by our leopard. I was about to mention this to Ubusuku when, as he stepped clear of the falls, he was knocked into the pool by the leopard as it sprang on him from an overhanging fig tree. As they sank, a bright red blot widened on the surface of the water. They came struggling to the surface, and the red blot was lost in white foam. The leopard was on Ubusuku's back, teeth sunk in the Zulu's right shoulder muscles.

They were less than six feet from me when I shoved my rifle muzzle against the leopard's side and pulled the trigger. The bolt snapped home on an empty chamber. Tears of chagrin ran down my face.

Ubusuku reached up and back, grabbed the leopard by the scruff of the neck, and dived under the surface. For a moment or two I couldn't see what was happening. When my eyes cleared I saw that Ubusuku still held the leopard's neck and that the leopard's teeth were still sunk in Ubusuku's shoulder.

The water was pink with blood. Man and beast were both gasping, and bubbles streamed from their mouths. They were suddenly almost still. I loaded my rifle, laid it at the pool's edge, and leaped to Ubusuku's aid. Even as I jumped, the leopard, a huge, half-drowned cat, crawled out of the pool and disappeared.

Ubusuku's arms and legs jerked weakly. White bubbles still darted upward from his half-open lips. I dragged him out and began giving first aid. Suddenly he pushed me, sat up, and said hoarsely:

"I talk to my *ehlose* [guardian spirit], *Baas*. Where is leopard? I kill him."

He got to his feet, swaying, eyes coal-black.

I said: "You gotta get medicine in those tooth holes. We gotta make quick to the outspan."

Without a word he ducked into the brush. I yelled. No answer. I picked up my rifle and, scared as hell, followed him. I knew from the look in his eyes that he intended to kill that leopard with his bare hands.

Ubusuku was like an elephant in his facility for pushing through dense brush silently and quickly. I had little hope of catching up with him, but I had to try.

Like his father, Indhlova, Ubusuku was a man of cold, relentless anger when his fierce Zulu pride was humbled. The leopard had certainly humbled it. Either the leopard or Ubusuku would now have to die.

Nearing the upper end of the *kloof*, I noticed blood shoulder-high on a branch. Ubusuku's blood.

Through thinning brush I began to get occasional glimpses of the bare, weathered, brown-red *kloof* walls. Abruptly there were no more trees. Only scattered bushes wrapped in spiraling yellow vines. A steep, narrow, rock-strewn ledge began where the creek was born from a bubbling spring.

Half a dozen steps along the ledge an adder lay writhing, its head partially crushed, lower jaw twisted at right angles to the upper one. A foot or so beyond was a big blob of blood where Ubusuku had paused to stamp the snake's head with his heel.

I put the snake out of its misery, then searched the cliff wall ahead. My eye was attracted by slight movement on top of an overhanging rock about fifty yards ahead. It was the big leopard, crouched to spring downward. I fired as he jumped and heard the satisfying thud of bullet striking flesh.

I reloaded as I ran. The leopard, shot through heart and lungs, lay on the ledge as if sleeping. Close beside him, Ubusuku knelt, his head and elbows on the ground. Blood still oozed darkly from a nest of teeth marks on his shoulder. He was unconscious.

Later he told me he had become weak and was forced to crawl. He didn't remember passing out.

The leopard? Its skin, skull, and feet were bought by the Natura Artis Magistra Society of Amsterdam, and for many years the mounted body was displayed in one of the buildings in the society's gardens.

When Jones and I finished pumping antiseptic into Ubusuku, I said: "We were lucky after all."

Jones scowled. "Ain't no luck." He looked keenly at me from beneath heavy gray brows.

"You done good," he said.

In the middle of that night, I sat up, cursing under my breath. We had forgotten to bring back our tiger fish.